THE BEGINNER'S GUIDE TO
MAKING POTTERY

THE BEGINNER'S GUIDE TO
MAKING POTTERY

BLITZ EDITIONS

Published by Blitz Editions
an imprint of Bookmart Ltd
Registered Number 2372865
Trading as Bookmart Ltd
Desford Road
Enderby
Leicester LE9 5AD

ISBN: 1 85605 312 1

Material previously published in 1992 as part of the encyclopedia set
Be Creative (Fabbri Publishing Ltd)

Editorial and design:
Brown Packaging Ltd,
255–257 Liverpool Road,
London N1 1LX

Printed in the Slovak Republic
60022

CONTENTS

SECTION ONE:

Working with Self-hardening Clay

A Mexican Bowl	7
Mirror Frame	11
Wall Vase	15
Nightlight Holder	21

SECTION TWO:

Working with Plaster and Clay

Moulded Tiles	27
Bas-relief Medallion	31
Cast Bookends	37
Plaster Bird	43
Draped Figure	49
Coiled Clay Pot	55
Candleholders	61
Clay Head	67

A MEXICAN BOWL

To make the bowl shown *below left,* you will need the following materials and equipment:

Above, a clean, smooth lint-free cloth (a teatowel or piece of sheeting, for example); a wooden rolling pin; rolling pin guides — slats of wood 5mm thick; clingfilm; an enamel basin of approximately 17cm in diameter and 7.5cm in depth; a 23-25cm plate; 1kg self-hardening clay; a potter's knife; modelling tools; a small natural sponge and bowl of water; a polythene bag.

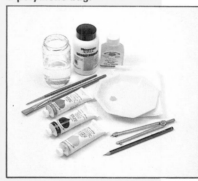

For applying the finish, *above,* 250ml acrylic gesso primer; a pair of compasses; an HB pencil for marking out the design; 60ml tubes of acrylic paint in the following colours: cadmium yellow, cadmium red and mars black; a jam jar of water; size 4 round nylon and ¾ inch flat nylon paint brushes; 75ml acrylic gloss varnish.

Handling and shaping clay satisfies a primitive instinct in all of us, and for those with creative abilities the urge to model in clay is particularly strong. For beginners with no access to a kiln, self-hardening or synthetic air-drying modelling materials are the ideal medium. Here we show you how to use this material to make an attractive bowl decorated with a vibrant Mexican frieze.

Special self-hardening clay brings the art of pottery to the hands of those who do not have access to a kiln. There are several types available — the off-white clay used here can be bought at most good art suppliers and craft outlets. Similar clay is also available through a few specialists; although it is less readily available, it is easier to work, and handles more like clays which have to be fired.

For a simple bowl, the easiest method of modelling the clay is to roll it out and shape it inside a suitable mould — in this case an enamel pudding basin. The clay is rolled out like pastry, using an ordinary rolling pin. The only specialist tools needed are a potter's knife with a fine blade and a couple of modelling tools with curved ends for smoothing the clay.

The surface of the hardened bowl is sealed with acrylic gesso primer to prevent the paint from soaking into the surface of the clay. The pattern is then drawn on and the bowl painted and decorated with tough acrylic paints. A final coat of varnish gives your bowl a high gloss finish.

PROJECT

MAKING THE BOWL

2 Using a 23-25cm plate as a guide, cut out a circle of clay using the potter's knife. Put the scraps into the polythene bag with the remaining clay. Line the enamel basin with clingfilm to prevent the clay from sticking to it, leaving about 6-10cm overlap all round. Lift the clay circle gently into the basin. It will form pleats so dip your fingers in water and use them to flatten the pleats out, working from the bottom of the basin upwards.

1 Take about 1kg of clay and put it on a clean cloth laid out over a board or work surface. Pat the clay out into a circular shape. Keep any remaining clay wrapped in polythene. Position the rolling pin guides on either side, about 25cm apart, and roll out the clay until it spreads to the guides, with the rolling pin touching the guides. Turn the clay from time to time so that it remains circular.

3 Using a damp sponge, smooth out the surface of the clay inside the bowl, working from the bottom upwards. Rinse out the sponge regularly. The surplus clay will form a frill around the top of the bowl. Trim this level with the top of the bowl using the potter's knife. Smooth the cut edge of the clay with a damp sponge.

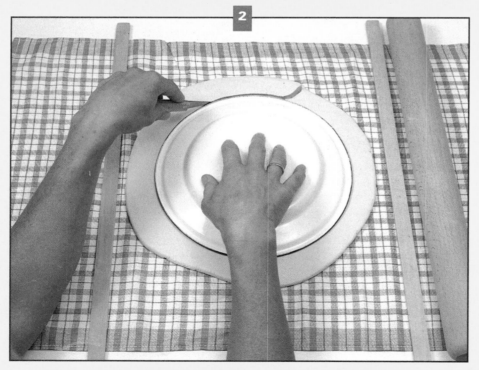

4 Take a small piece of the remaining clay, about the size of a walnut, and roll it out to form a sausage (known as a coil). It must be long enough to go around the top of the bowl, with an overlap of 5mm-1cm.

5 Dampen the clay around the top of the bowl and lay the coil all around to form a lip. Trim off the excess clay and butt the ends together. Seal the lip to the bowl around the inside, using a modelling tool to merge a little of the clay from the coil with the bowl. Smooth over the join with a damp cloth.

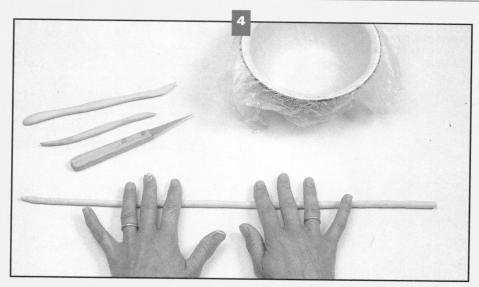

6 Finish off the outer edge of the lip as shown, running the end of a modelling tool around the bowl between the lip and the basin. Leave the clay to harden for 1-3 hours before removing the bowl from the basin (it should still be soft on the outside).

7 Lift the bowl out of the basin using the clingfilm. Turn the basin upside down and cover the outside with clingfilm. Carefully fit the bowl over the outside of the basin. Smooth the surface of the clay with a modelling tool, followed by a damp sponge, to remove the marks left by the clingfilm. Leave to harden for an hour or two, then remove from the basin and leave to dry out.

The frieze design, *right*, is shown actual size, so you can use it to measure the distance of the horizontal lines from the top of the pot (top of picture) when you are marking out the design on your bowl.

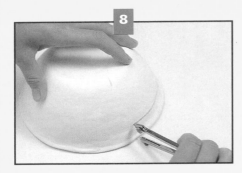

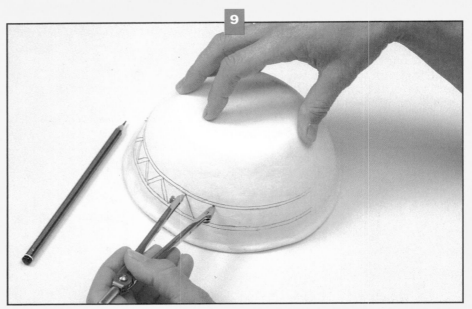

8 Paint the bowl inside and out with a coat of acrylic gesso primer to seal the surface. When this is dry, put the bowl upside down on a work surface (a banding wheel, potter's wheel or cake icing turntable are ideal). Using the pattern *above* as a guide, measure the distance of the first horizontal line from the top of the bowl and mark on the pot. With compasses, and turning the bowl on your wheel, draw the first line right round the bowl, then repeat the process for the second, third and fourth lines.

9 Mark the position of the zig-zag lines by marking dots on the inner parallel lines. Join the dots to make the zig-zag lines. Mark the circles in the centre of the triangles.

10 Using an old plate as a palette, squeeze out some yellow paint. Wet the brush in a small bowl of clean water and paint the inside of the bowl. Wash the brush and leave the paint to dry. Paint in the black with the flat brush, using horizontal strokes and leaving the frieze white. Wash the brush, then use the size 4 brush to paint in the black triangles, leaving the circles and bands unpainted. Wash the brush, then paint in first the red lines, then the yellow dots. Leave to dry overnight. Finally, apply two coats of varnish.

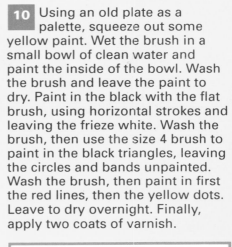

Your Mexican bowl will be quite durable, and you can wipe it clean with a damp cloth (but don't attempt to immerse it in water). You could use it as a fruit bowl, or keep an arrangement of dried flowers in it.

MODELLING

MIRROR FRAME

In the first modelling project we introduced you to self-hardening clay and showed you how to shape it into a bowl using a mould. This project uses clay in a completely different way to create a colourful frame for a mirror.

This decorative mirror frame is built up by joining rolled slabs of clay together. To ensure that the whole thing is securely constructed it is important to make strong joins at all stages. To do this, all pieces to be joined are moistened with water and pressed firmly together. The joins are then smoothed over with a modelling tool to seal any gaps. For the two large pieces (the back and front of the frame) the surfaces to be joined are scored first to give a better grip.

The leaves, berries and stems that decorate the frame are all cut out or modelled individually and carefully stuck on. This takes time, so don't try to rush it. There is much satisfaction and enjoyment to be had from working in clay, and it is the painstaking application of the decoration that will give you a successful result. Remember to store any unused clay in an airtight polythene bag for your next project.

Shrinking clay
A certain amount of shrinkage will occur as the clay dries, so don't take your measurements for the mirror until the frame has completely dried out.

MATERIALS

To make the mirror frame *below left* you will need:

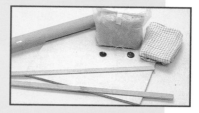

Above, 2kg self-hardening clay; a wooden rolling pin; rolling pin guides (2 slats of wood 5mm thick); a wooden board at least 25 x 36cm; a clean, smooth lint-free cloth (ie teatowel or piece of sheet); clay cutting wire (or length of monofilament nylon such as fishing line with a button fixed at each end).

Above, cartridge paper at least 25 x 36cm; pencil; metal ruler; craft knife; modelling tools and modelling knife; hardener; polythene bag; 5cm length of wire at least 2mm in diameter.

Above, soft towel; acrylic gesso primer; water jar and water; palette or saucer; acrylic paints (azo yellow-orange; light green oxide and titanium white); acrylic gloss varnish; size 4 and size 1 round and ¾ inch flat nylon brushes; mirror approximately 115 x 140mm; roll of electrical insulating tape; picture wire; scissors.

PROJECT

THE TEMPLATES

Front

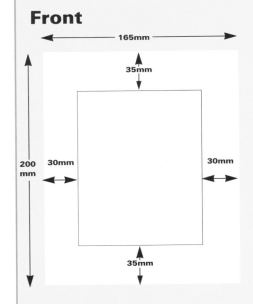

165mm

35mm

200 mm

30mm

30mm

35mm

Back

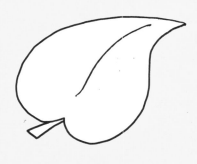

On cartridge paper, draw up the templates for the back and front of the frame to the measurements given, and make a template for the leaf by tracing from the outline shown. Enlarge the design for the mirror decoration on a photocopier to a width of 175mm at the widest point. Mark the top of the design clearly (the leaves on the sides point upwards).

165mm

30mm

200 mm

25 mm

25 mm

30mm

TOP

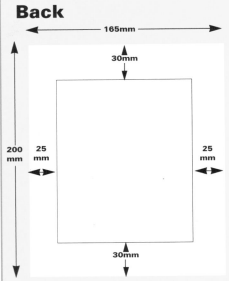

1 Spread a clean cloth on a work surface and place the rolling guides about 28cm apart. Using a clay cutting wire, cut a piece of clay about 5 x 10 x 17cm and place

on the cloth. Roll the clay out with the rolling pin until it is level with the rolling guides (ie 5mm thick).

2 Put the templates you have drawn for the back and front of the frame on a board and cut them out using a craft knife and a metal ruler. Position the templates on the clay and cut out the pieces with a modelling knife, using a rolling guide as a ruler. Store the remaining clay and any scraps in a polythene bag to prevent it drying out. Leave the pieces of the frame to harden for an hour.

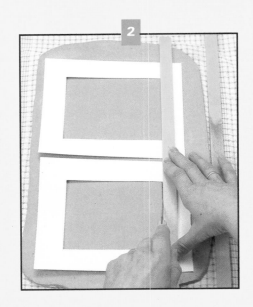

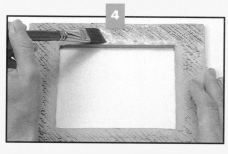

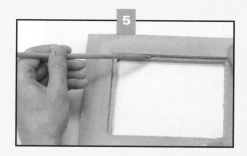

3 Place the frame pieces on the board and use the modelling knife to score the surface of both pieces, leaving a border of 5mm unscored on the inside edge of the front piece (the piece with the smaller cut out centre).

4 Using the flat nylon brush, wet the scored surfaces with water.

5 Place the back of the frame on top of the front (wet surfaces together), carefully lining up the outside edges. Press down firmly to seal. Smooth all the joins with a modelling tool.

6 Carefully turn the frame over and neaten the edges with a modelling knife, cutting at a slight angle along the edge of the back piece (as shown).

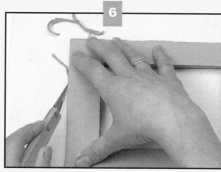

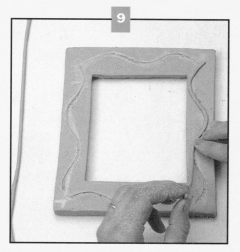

7 Turn the frame over again and smooth the edges with wet fingers. Then make the holes for the hanging wire by carefully pushing a curved piece of wire through one layer of clay in the two positions shown.

8 Turn the frame over to work on the front. Smooth all the edges carefully with wet fingers. Place the drawing of the design over the frame, making sure that the top is at the end with the hanging holes. Trace over the drawing with a modelling tool to mark the position of the stems.

9 Remove the drawing and score the stem lines more deeply with a modelling tool. Roll out with your hands four thin coils of clay about 20cm long and 2-3mm in diameter. Brush water on to the scored lines, and place the coils in the grooves. Seal the joins with a modelling tool.

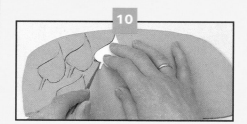

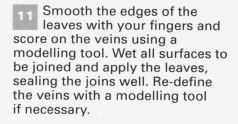

10 Roll out some clay for the leaves to about 3-4mm thick, cut out the template for the leaf and cut out 18 leaves using the modelling knife.

11 Smooth the edges of the leaves with your fingers and score on the veins using a modelling tool. Wet all surfaces to be joined and apply the leaves, sealing the joins well. Re-define the veins with a modelling tool if necessary.

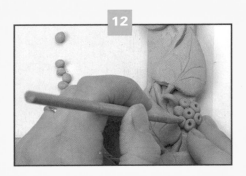

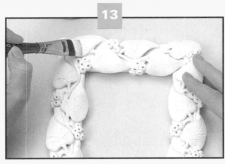

12 Roll some small coils of clay for the stalks of the berries. For the berries roll tiny balls of clay in the palm of one hand using the index finger of the other hand. Attach the stalks in the usual way. Wet the frame where you wish to position the berries and press them down firmly. Use the modelling tool to make the dot in the centre — this helps to secure the berries.

13 Leave the frame to dry thoroughly for about 2 days. Then seal with hardener, mixed

according to the manufacturer's instructions, using a 3/4 inch flat brush. Alternatively, dry the frame in an oven for 1 hour 30 minutes at 50ºC, rising to 100ºC for a further hour (if you use an oven there is no need to seal with hardener). Using the 3/4 inch flat brush, paint the frame with white acrylic primer, switching to a size 4 round brush to paint in between the berries and leaves. Leave to dry for 30 minutes. Remember to wash your brushes in water immediately after using acrylic paints as they dry very fast.

14 Mix a pale green paint using the green with a little azo yellow-orange and titanium white. Using a size 4 and size 1 round brush, paint the stems, then leave to dry.

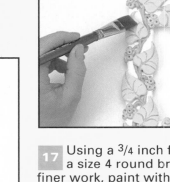

17 Using a 3/4 inch flat brush and a size 4 round brush for the finer work, paint with two coats of varnish, leaving the frame to dry for 2-4 hours between coats. Leave to dry thoroughly.

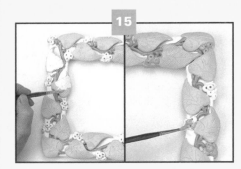

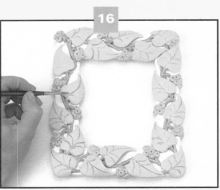

15 Mix roughly equal proportions of azo yellow-orange and titanium white and, using the size 4 round brush, paint all the leaves, then add a little more yellow-orange to the mix and paint the berries. Leave to dry.

16 Using a size 1 brush, pick out the leaf veins and centres of the berries using the same green mix you used for the stems. Leave to dry.

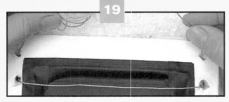

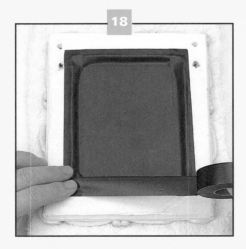

18 Turn the frame over and put it on a soft towel to protect the front. Measure the mirror recess at the back, then take the measurements to a glazier and have a piece of mirror cut to size. Our mirror is approximately 115 x 140mm. Place the mirror, reflective side down, in the frame and secure the joins with strips of electrical insulating tape.

19 Cut a length of picture wire with scissors, then thread it through the hanging holes and knot securely.

MODELLING

WALL VASE

MATERIALS

To make the wall vase shown *below left* you will need:

Above, 1kg plasticine; piece of thick dowel or rolling pin; cotton cloth, such as a tea towel; modelling tools, Das T3191 and Das wire modelling tool; 1kg self-hardening clay; knife; one multi-purpose cooking bag, polythene sandwich or freezer bag; petroleum jelly; cocktail stick or very sharp pencil; sharpened lolly stick; ruler; wooden board.

Above, tracing paper; carbon paper; pencil; gesso; No 3 and No 5 artist's brushes; No 12 brush, for varnishing; palette; poster and watercolour varnish; designers gouache in the following colours — Naples yellow, primary yellow, spectrum red; permanent green deep; spectrum violet; black; white.

For this lesson in modelling a three-dimensional object we have used a plasticine mould and self-hardening clay. The inspiration for our wall vase came from a type of pottery popular in the 1940s and 1950s that is sometimes referred to as 'Fairground' pottery.

Fairground pottery was made from inexpensive plaster and decorated with bright colours. Although scorned by some collectors, it has a distinct charm of its own and can look very attractive when various objects — flowers in baskets, birds and butterflies — are grouped on a wall.

Our vase is formed over a plasticine mould, so if you remove the mould carefully from the clay you will be able to use it again. It is particularly important to remove the vase from the mould before it dries;

otherwise the clay will crack. Removing the mould is the only difficult procedure in making the vase, and requires patience and careful handling.

The clay is not entirely waterproof, even when varnished thoroughly, so it is not advisable to put water and real flowers into it. However, you can use your vase to hold an arrangement of dried flowers. You will find a great variety of dried flowers in the shops in all colours — so choose a selection that tone well with the colours of the vase.

USING THE TEMPLATE

Photocopy the template at 150%. Put a piece of carbon paper under the tracing paper and go over the design with a pencil.

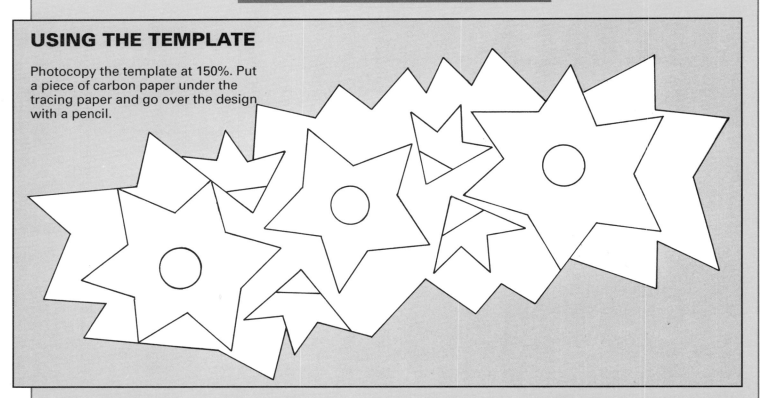

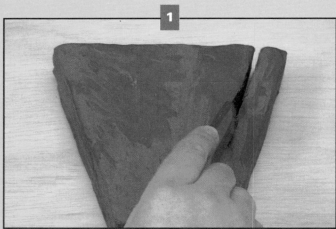

1 To make the mould for your vase, place the plasticine on a board and form it into a square approximately 140 x 140mm. Using the diagram *below* as a guide, roughly mould your square to the dimensions and shape of the vase, keeping the surface as smooth as possible as you work. Use a craft knife to model the bottom and sides, as shown.

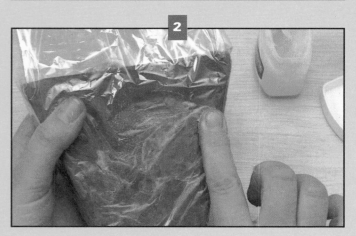

2 Place the mould in a polythene bag and wrap the excess polythene neatly around it, leaving at least 150mm free at the top of the mould. This will help you to pull the mould from the clay at a later stage. Smother the bag with petroleum jelly.

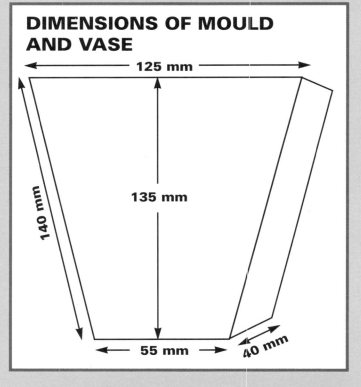

DIMENSIONS OF MOULD AND VASE

125 mm

140 mm

135 mm

55 mm

40 mm

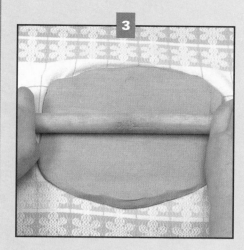

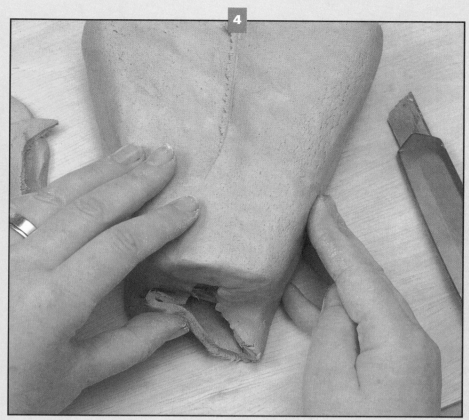

3 Roll out some clay on a cotton tea towel with a piece of dowel until it measures 370 x 150mm and is 5mm thick. Cut straight along the top and bottom so that the width of the clay is 360 x 14mm.

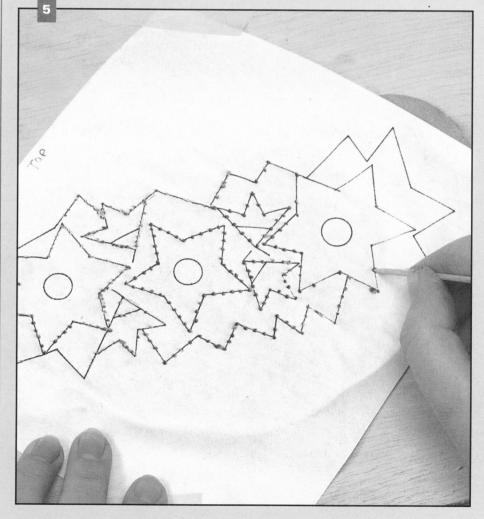

4 Place the mould on a board and wrap the clay around the mould. Press the clay into the shape of the mould by cutting straight down the two outside edges, then bringing the outside edges to the centre, overlapping them a little. Blend the edges together with your fingers — wetting your fingers with water if necessary — and smooth the edges to get rid of the 'seam'. Fold the clay up over the bottom of the mould, as shown, to make the base. You may need to cut away the extra clay. Again, smooth and fit with your fingers and water. Cover the vase with a damp cloth.

5 Roll out more clay on the tea towel to make a rectangle approximately 250 x 110mm and 2.5mm thick. Place your template on to the clay. Using the sharp end of a cocktail stick or very sharp pencil go over all the lines, 'pricking' the paper with small dots placed close together. Just mark the centres of the three circles — you don't have to draw around them as the circles are added later. Lift up the template occasionally to see if you are applying enough pressure.

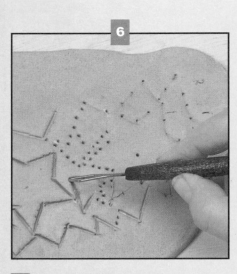

6 Remove the template and indent the lines of the flowers with the wire tool.

7 Cut around the perimeter of the flowers using the wooden modelling tool, as shown.

8 Score the surface of the vase where the decoration will be placed and wet this area with a brush to make the clay 'gluey'.

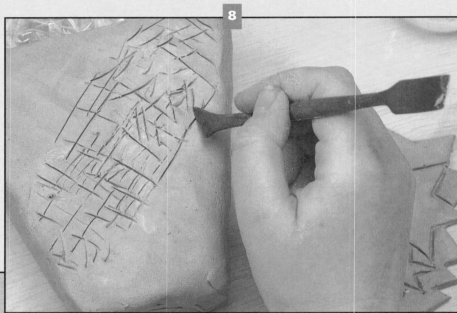

9 Lay the vase flat and gently place the flower shapes on it. With the modelling tools and a brush, firm around the edges so that no lines can be seen. If necessary, use some more wet clay to cover the join, and continue to press the decorative area down on to the vase.

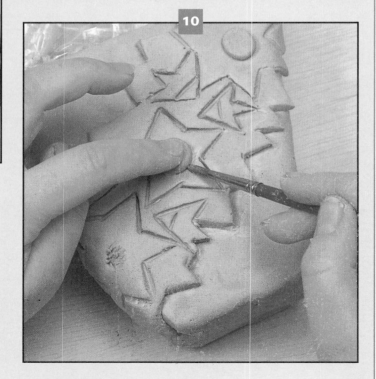

10 Re-draw the lines with tools where necessary. Take three pieces of clay the size of large peas and roll them into ball, then press them flat. Score the centre of each flower and add water with a brush. Press the flattened circles firmly in place and smooth with water and fingers.

11 Roll out two sections of clay approximately 150 x 30mm and 2.5mm thick. Draw a zig-zag pattern 10mm across on each one with a sharp point. Cut out the zig-zag patterns with the tool as neatly as possible. Score the areas at the top and bottom of the vase where the zig-zag patterns will go. Wet the clay and place the zig-zags in place. Neaten with water and the pointed end of a tool or knife.

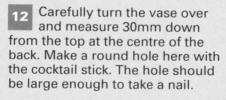

12 Carefully turn the vase over and measure 30mm down from the top at the centre of the back. Make a round hole here with the cocktail stick. The hole should be large enough to take a nail.

13 Allow the vase to become leather dry (this takes about three to four hours). Do not leave it until it shrinks and cracks or it will become difficult to remove the mould. Gently run a knife around the top of the vase to loosen it and carefully pull the plastic and plasticine away. Using your fingers and some water, smooth the rim of the vase and any other dents that may have occurred. Smooth inside too. Leave to dry for about two days.

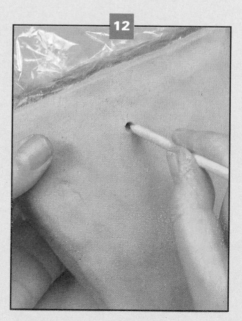

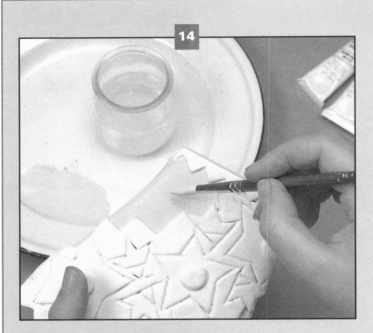

COLOUR GUIDE

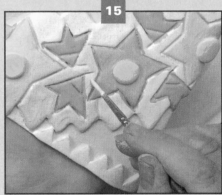

DG Dark green (permanent green deep)
LG Light green (permanent green deep + white)
Y Yellow (primary yellow)
C Cream (Naples yellow + white)

B Black
P Pink (spectrum red + white)
PP Pale pink (spectrum red + white)
M Mauve (spectrum violet + white)

14 When the vase is dry, paint the inside and the outside with gesso (you may find this easier if you mix a little water in with the gesso). Allow two to three hours for the gesso to dry. Then paint the inside and all of the outside of the vase cream, with the exception of the flower border. Mix a good quantity of the cream colour, as you will need quite a lot.

15 Paint the flowers, following the colour guide. Leave to dry thoroughly, then varnish with poster and gouache varnish.

If you wish, design your own decoration for the vase. For inspiration it is worth going to local museums or, if you are visiting London, go to the Victoria and Albert Museum where you will see a wealth of designs, patterns and colours used to decorate pottery throughout different periods in history.

MODELLING

NIGHTLIGHT HOLDER

MATERIALS

To make the nightlight holder shown *below left* you will need:

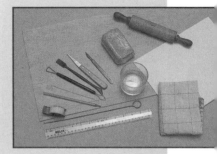

Above, 1¹/₂kg Newclay (or any self-hardening clay); cotton tea towel; spatula-type and wire-ended modelling tools; modelling knife; rolling pin; ruler; wooden board; A4 thin card; glass (for mould) 7.5cm diameter, 10cm high; adhesive tape; cocktail stick; skewer.

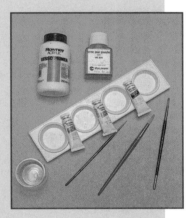

Above, acrylic gesso; designer's gouache in gold, Prussian blue, cobalt pale hue; palette; jam jar; paintbrushes, sizes 3, 5, 12; non-flammable varnish.

We use self-hardening clay to make this decorative nightlight holder — when the nightlight is lit after dark, the cut-out stars twinkle alluringly against a bright background.

Our nightlight holder is designed to look decorative both unlit in daylight, and after dark with a candle nightlight burning inside. The three cut-out stars give out a warm, romantic glow, ideal for lighting a patio after dark.

We have used Newclay to make our nightlight holder. This is a type of self-hardening clay that contains minute nylon fibres to strengthen it. This makes the finished pot very strong, but it does mean that the surface may not be perfectly smooth, as the fibres tend to stick out.

The pot is modelled by wrapping rolled out clay round a glass tumbler. Thin card is wrapped round the glass mould first, and secured with adhesive tape. This makes it easier to remove the clay later.

When you are painting the nightlight holder, remember to mix up enough of the background colour to paint all over the inside and outside. Mix the paint thick enough to give good cover — the consistency of double cream is about right. Inspect the pot carefully while you are painting to make sure that all the awkward angles of the cut-out stars have been covered.

HELPFUL HINT

You can obtain self-hardening clay from most good art shops and craft outlets. Modelling tools are also available from the same sources, but you could improvise with sticks, pieces of wire and small household knives.

P R O J E C T

TEMPLATES
for stars

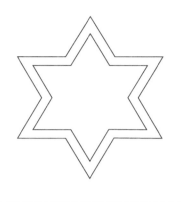

1 Photocopy the templates for the stars at original size. Rub over the back of the design with pencil and, with a pencil, trace three large and three small stars separately on to thin card. Cut out the six stars using a scalpel and ruler.

2 Cut a piece of card to fit around the glass tumbler as tightly as possible and to extend beyond the height of the glass by about 6cm. Take a measurement of the circumference of the glass (here, 27cm) from the card before joining the edges together with adhesive tape to make a smooth join.

3 Roll out some clay to 5mm thick and cut a piece 28 x 10cm using a ruler and a pointed tool.

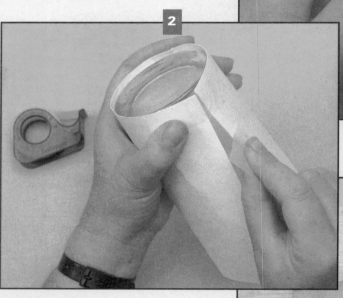

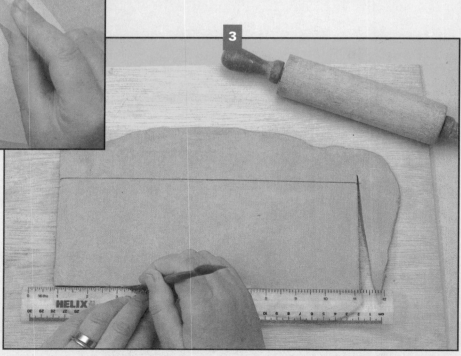

DESIGN GUIDE (all dimensions given in centimetres)

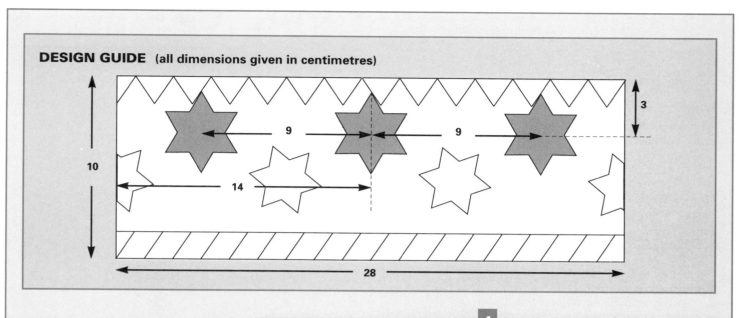

4 Using the design guide, lightly mark the centre points of the cut-out (shaded) stars with a pencil on the clay. Place the three large star templates on these points and score around them with a cocktail stick. Carefully cut out the shapes with the modelling knife and remove them. Smooth the cut edges with the knife blade and your fingers.

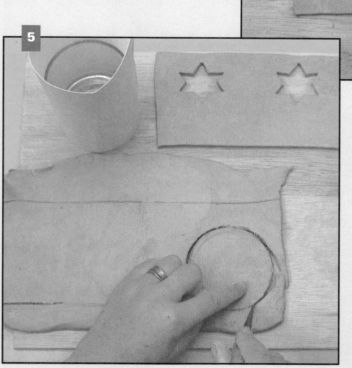

5 Roll out a piece of clay to a thickness of 6mm and place the glass on the clay. Score around the base of the glass with the knife, leaving a margin of about 3mm. Cut out the circle.

6 Wrap the rectangle of clay around the glass and trim the overlap down to about 3mm.

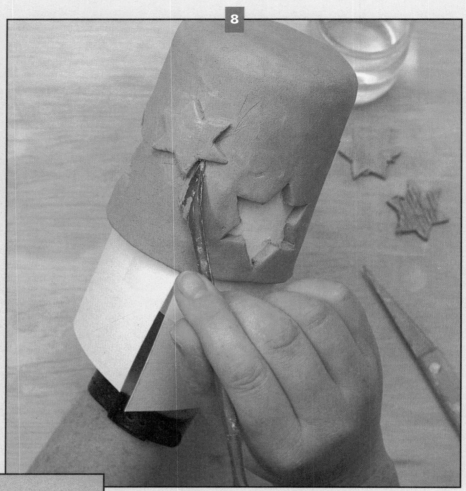

7 Place the base in position and join it to the sides, moulding the join smooth with your fingers and wetting the clay with water. Smooth the side join in the same way.

8 Roll out a strip of clay to a thickness of 5mm and cut out three stars using the smaller star template. Cut two strips of clay 1.5cm wide for the borders. Score the backs of the stars and attach them to the clay (see the design guide on page 23), wetting the clay with water. Smooth the edges.

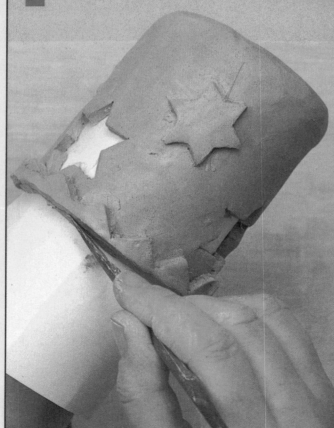

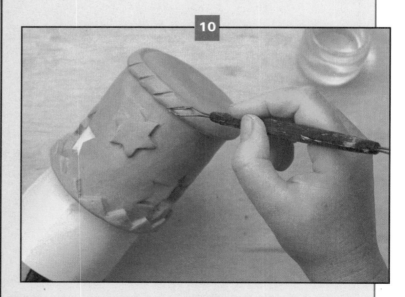

9 With a knife, cut one edge of one of the border strips into triangular shapes, score and dampen the surfaces and stick to the rim. Smooth the edges.

10 Join the other border strip to the bottom of the pot in the same way. Using the wire tool, make angled indentations at 1cm intervals.

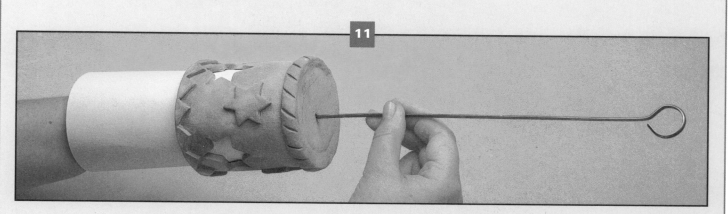

11

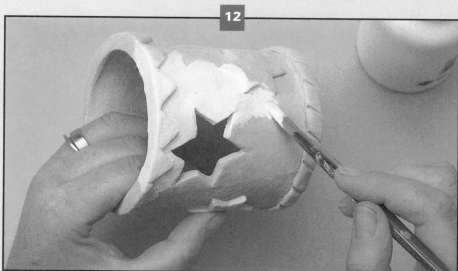

12

11 Leave the pot to dry for about 1½ hours until hard. Ease the glass out of the clay by pushing a skewer through the base. Remove the card. Fill the hole in the base with a little plug of clay, and smooth the inside edges of the pot with a modelling tool and a wet sponge.

12 Smooth all surfaces and edges as much as possible, taking care to get rid of all the fibres which tend to stick out. Leave the pot to dry completely for about two days. Apply a coat of gesso inside and out, and leave to dry.

13

13 Mix a generous quantity of cobalt pale hue gouache and paint the background areas of the outside of the pot (see colour guide, *right*) and the cut edges of the stars. When dry, paint the inside.

COLOUR GUIDE

PB — Prussian blue
G — gold
C — cobalt pale hue

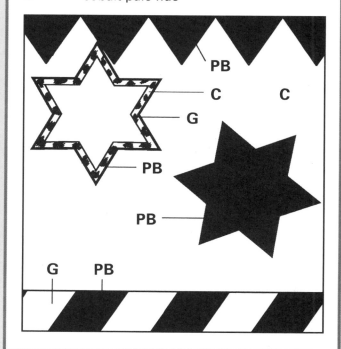

14 Paint the areas indicated with Prussian blue. Paint the bands on the top of the rim (see *right*) with a fairly dry brush to give a textured look.

15 Finally, paint the gold spots around the cut-out stars and the gold areas on the base border. When the pot is completely dry, varnish inside and out.

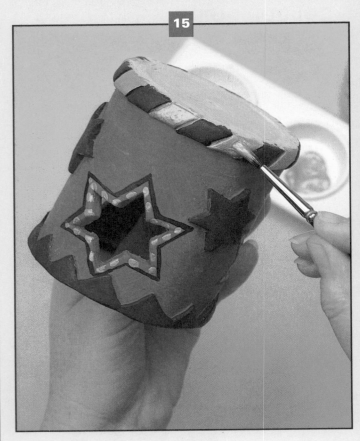

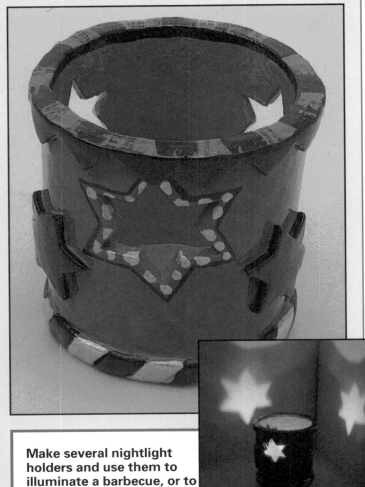

Make several nightlight holders and use them to illuminate a barbecue, or to create attractive table lights instead of candles for an indoor dinner party.

SCULPTURE AND 3-D

MOULDED TILES

Above, a non-porous work board or sheet of polythene; felt-tip pen; 1 kilo clay; a rolling pin or piece of dowelling; two pieces of wood for rolling guides, 15mm deep and at least 200mm long; a steel ruler; set square; 6 wooden laths 22 x 5mm and 150mm long; 6 wooden laths 160mm long.

Above, nuts or other items to embed in the clay; petroleum jelly; 1 kilo plaster of Paris; mixing bowl; water.

Plaster casting is one of the most complex techniques used by professional sculptors. But the principles are simple, and these moulded relief tiles with food motifs make a good introduction to the basic method of casting with plaster.

These decorative wall tiles for the kitchen are cast in plaster directly from a bed of clay in which an impression has been made. This is the simplest method of casting a 3-dimensional form.

Clay and plaster have entirely different characteristics, and it is this difference that enables them to work together in the casting process. Clay is malleable and therefore easily modelled. To keep it soft, it must be tightly wrapped in polythene when you are not using it. If it is left exposed to the air it will soon dry out and become unusable.

Plaster (usually plaster of Paris) is a gypsum which has been heated so that it loses 75% of its water content. The re-introduction of water activates a chemical process so that the powdered plaster of Paris is turned into a creamy paste before returning to a brittle solid. Plaster of Paris is available

from chemists and specialist suppliers.

Once mixed with water the plaster must be used immediately because it will begin to set within 15 minutes, although it takes longer to harden fully. You can tell when it is beginning to set because the chemical reaction with the water gives off heat, so the plaster will warm as it sets. Our tiles will set in about 20 minutes, but leave them for at least 2 hours to harden fully.

Painting and finishing
Plain white plaster is not very durable so it needs to be finished in some way. We have primed these plaster tiles with white primer and painted them with colourful water-based acrylic paints. They can be coated with varnish for a glossy finish. For a white finish you could simply prime and varnish.

Above, water jar and water, water-based acrylic paints in red, yellow, emerald, blue and white; round size 7 brush.

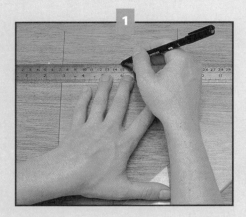

1 Mark a 150mm square in the centre of the rolling surface, projecting the guide lines to the edge of the board.

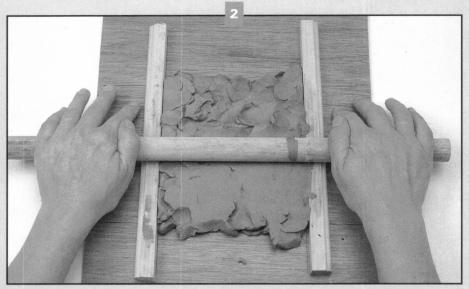

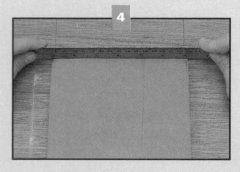

2 Position the rolling guides on opposite sides of the square. Take a lump of clay about the size of a small melon and roll it out on the rolling surface until it fills the space between the rolling guides and covers the marked square. The clay should make a block 150 x 160mm.

3 Level the surface of the clay by dragging the steel ruler across it. Alternatively, you can give some background texture by dabbing the surface with a sponge, sweeping a brush across it, or pressing coarsely woven fabric on to the surface to leave an impression.

4 Use the ruler to trim the clay block so that it is exactly 150mm square.

5 Enclose the clay square with 4 laths. Seal the angle between the work board and the laths, and the corners where the laths meet, with wet clay. This stops the plaster leaking out.

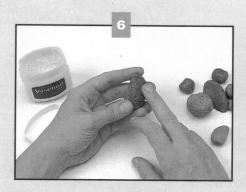

6 Cover the side of the first object to be impressed into the clay with a thin layer of petroleum jelly to prevent it from sticking to the clay.

7 Press the object into the clay to make a deep impression and remove carefully without disturbing the surrounding clay. Repeat with other objects to form a design.

MIXING PLASTER

HELPFUL HINT

Mixing plaster takes a little practice and requires precise timing.

• Put 500ml water in a large bowl. You will need to add up to 2 parts plaster (by volume) to 1 part water.
• Sprinkle the plaster over the water.
• Allow the plaster to sink to the bottom

of the bowl of water — do not stir.
• Continue sprinkling the plaster on to the water until a handful or so floats on the surface instead of sinking.

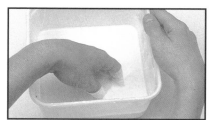

• Plunge your hand in and mix the plaster thoroughly, ensuring that there are no lumps. It should have the consistency of double cream.

The plaster is now ready to pour and will solidify in as little as 15 minutes.

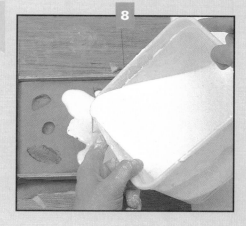

8 Mix the plaster (see box, *left*) and pour it evenly over the clay to just below the rim of the wooden laths.

9 While the plaster is still creamy, jog the frame gently to ensure the plaster reaches the crevices of the clay impressions, and to level the surface of the plaster. Leave to harden for at least 2 hours.

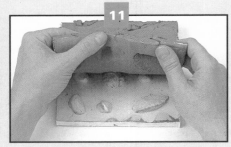

10 Remove the laths, then gently lever the plaster and clay off the board.

11 Turn the tile over and remove the clay.

12 To remove the residual clay, wash the plaster tile in cold water, brushing with a soft brush if necessary. Leave to dry out for another hour or so.

13 Prime the surface of the tile and allow to dry. Paint all over with the background colour, applying at least two coats, and allowing the paint to dry thoroughly between coats.

To make the asparagus tiles

To make the asparagus-tip tiles, use asparagus cut to a length of approximately 10cm, and 2 baby sweetcorn sliced in half. Press the asparagus and cut sections of the corn into the clay as in steps 6 and 7.

To paint the backgrounds of the tiles, use a mix of emerald and coeruleum blue, adding titanium white to lighten the tint. Use cadmium yellow mixed with white for the sweetcorn.

Paint the asparagus with a fairly dry brush, using various mixtures of emerald, coeruleum blue, titanium white and cadmium yellow to achieve a shaded effect. Finally, paint the tips of the asparagus with red violet.

14 Paint the relief areas in a contrasting colour, applying as many coats as necessary to build up the desired colour. Allow to dry between coats. Varnish with acrylic varnish if you wish.

You could make several of these decorative kitchen tiles with different motifs and use them among white tiles as a splashback for the sink. If varnished, they can be wiped clean with a damp cloth.

MODELLING

BAS-RELIEF MEDALLION

In the Moulded Tiles casting project, natural objects were used to make the plaster casts. Here we show you how to make a medallion by casting a modelled plasticine image. The modelling of the image gives you the opportunity to make a sculptural relief of the human body.

Some of the greatest artists in history have designed and cast medallions in bronze. A fine medallion can present a portrait or other image that is as sensitive as any painted likeness, but modelled on a very small scale. Medallions have served many purposes in the past and are still being made to commemorate marriages, births, prizes and historical events. They can therefore make a personal and intimate gift for a special occasion.

In this lesson you will learn how to make a one-sided medallion in plaster that can be regarded as a finished object in itself. Plaster is a versatile and satisfying material, and when finished with a natural varnish or a waterproofing material such as shellac it can look very beautiful.

If you wish to have a more durable medallion you can take your plaster version to an art foundry to be cast in bronze. Various methods are used for casting medallions, but one of the most frequently used is cire- perdue, or 'lost wax' casting. A wax model of the medallion has to be made

first, identical to the finished product. Art foundries can make this from a plaster model, by making a negative rubber mould or using your own negative plaster mould.

We have used plasticine as the modelling material for the image, but if you want a larger, more free-form bas-relief, you should use clay. If, however, the design has a lot of fine detail, then a better choice is modelling wax, obtainable from companies supplying materials for sculptors.

HELPFUL HINT

If you intend to do a lot of work using plaster casts you may find that you wish to fit a plaster trap under your sink unit. One of the problems with plaster is that it can be quite messy, and because it dries so fast, bowls, tools and hands need to be washed frequently. A plaster trap will prevent washed away plaster from clogging sink pipes and drains. Ask your plumber for further advice.

MATERIALS

For the medallion shown *below left* you will need:

Above, tracing paper; compass; pencil; perspex sheet, approximately 80mm square and 3mm thick; small fret saw; scissors.

Above, 80mm mill bastard file; two sheets of sandpaper, F2 and 320; wax modelling tools, 117 and 72; stainless steel dentist's tool SK; thick piece of dowel or rolling pin; packet of plasticine.

Above, 1 kg clay; piece of board for rolling clay; 1 kg plaster of Paris; two 25mm decorator's paint brushes; liquid detergent; small bowl; plastic container; bar of toilet soap.

Above, three table knives; sharp kitchen knife; small hammer; rasp; methylated spirits; 500g shellac flakes; small jar.

P R O J E C T

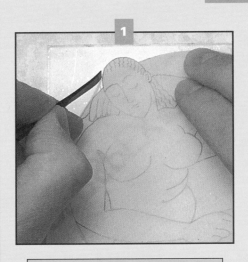

1 Enlarge the template to 200% and trace it on to tracing paper, using compasses to mark in the outside circle. Cut out the tracing. Using the pencil and compasses, draw the same size circle on to the perspex sheet. Heat the straightest end of modelling tool 117 and place the template on the perspex. Using the edge of the heated tip of the tool, draw the outline of the protruding head on to the perspex, as shown.

THE TEMPLATE

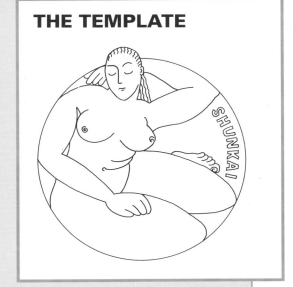

HELPFUL HINT

To heat the end of the modelling tool, hold it in a gas flame until it is hot enough to mark the perspex. You will have to test it on the perspex to see when it is hot enough, but make certain you do not mark inside the circle.

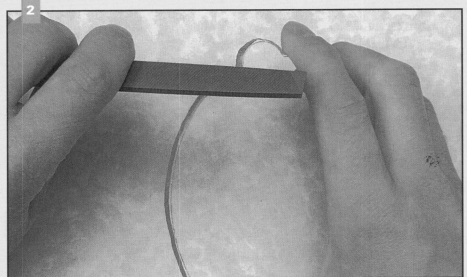

2 Cut out the design on the perspex with the fret saw, cutting about 1mm outside the lines. Using the coarser file first, and then the finer one, make a neat bevelled edge that comes up to the pencil line of the circle. Hold the file at an angle of about 60°.

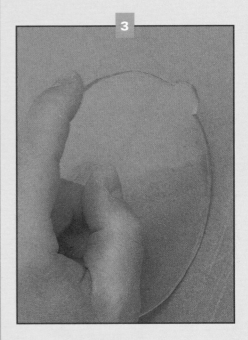

3 Sand the edges of the perspex with the two grades of sandpaper, again using the coarser paper first. For the best results, lay the sandpaper on your work surface and 'stroke' the edge of the perspex across it, drawing it towards you as you sand.

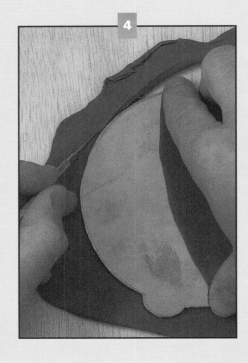

4 Roll out the plasticine on a board to a thickness of about 8mm (or the height of the highest area of relief you want to obtain). Turn the perspex circle upside down and place it on top of the plasticine. Using the dentist's tool as shown, cut out the plasticine. Use the bevelled edge of the perspex as your cutting guide to give a bevelled edge to your plasticine circle.

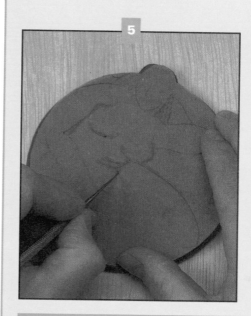

5 Turn the perspex and plasticine over and place your template on top of it, making certain the image is located accurately. Again using the dentist's tool, trace the image on to the plasticine, going over all the lines except for those for the hair and the lettering. It does not matter if you tear the paper template in places.

6 Remove the template and cut away all the areas that will be flat on the medallion.

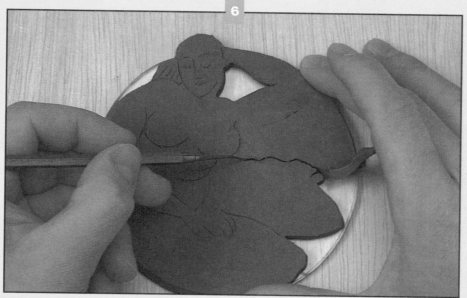

MODELLING

1 When modelling, be quite bold at first, cutting away the areas that will be lower and slicing off the plasticine at an angle to form the curves of the limbs. In so doing you create a strong and confident impression of the three-dimensional body you are trying to portray. Don't worry if the modelling looks quite angular at this point — this is to be expected.

2 Build up the image by adding bits of plasticine where necessary until you are satisfied with your modelled image.

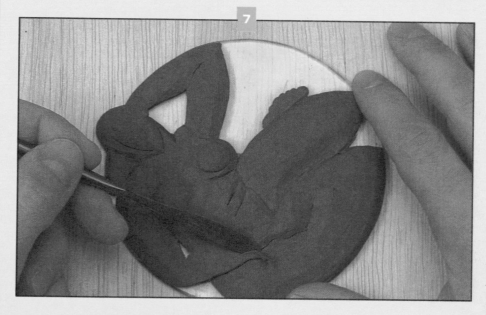

7 Model the plasticine with the modelling tools, making certain that you do not create any undercuts (see Modelling, *left*, and the diagrams *below*. The diagram *below left* is an undercut).

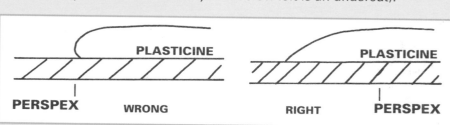

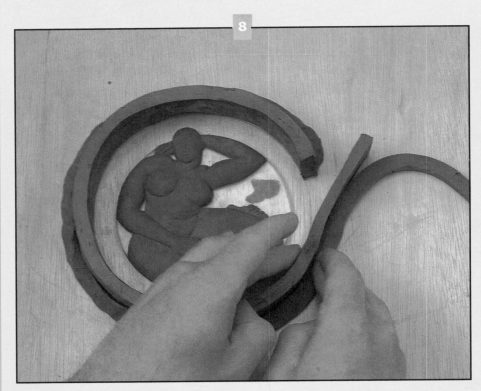

8 Draw a circle with a radius about 70mm on to the wooden board and place your plasticine model (which should still be attached to the perspex) exactly in the centre, using small bits of plasticine as 'glue' to secure it to the board. This will stop the medallion from sliding around when the plaster is poured on top. Roll out a strip of wet clay, about 10mm thick and 50mm wide, and use it to make a wall around the medallion, with the large circle as your guide. Make another small strip of wet clay to seal the wall to the board, as shown. Make certain that the wall is strong enough to withstand the bulk of liquid plaster. Smear a small amount of cooking oil or petroleum jelly on the board between the wall and the perspex.

9 Mix the same quantity of plaster as given for the moulded tiles on page 29, and pour an even layer of it over the medallion, shaking the board slightly to ensure that any bubbles rise to the top. Continue to pour until the plaster comes to a height of about 10mm above the highest point of the relief. Leave to harden for at least two hours.

10 Remove the clay wall and carefully lift the plaster cast off the board. With the V-shaped tool clean off the extra plaster from the perspex circle and carve a V-shape around the edge of the perspex. Carefully lift out the perspex and plasticine, as shown.

11 You will now be working in the negative, so turn your template upside-down and place it on the plaster relief, again making certain that it is centrally located. Draw in the hair and lettering using the dentist's tool.

12 Remove the template and carefully engrave the letters and hair, starting with a shallow cut and gradually making it deeper. Now is the time to perfect your modelling. You can smooth out any bumpy curves in the negative with fine sand paper and cut away any remaining undercuts. Immerse the plaster in water for at least half an hour.

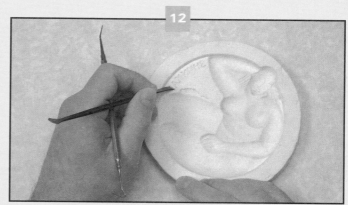

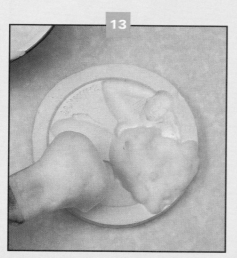

13 Remove the plaster and pat dry with a towel. Place a bar of soap in a bowl with about one thimble-full of water. Stir the soap and water vigorously with a paint brush to make a stiff foam with the consistency of a stiffly beaten egg white. Dab this on to the plaster negative and leave for six minutes.

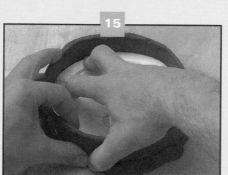

14 Place the plaster negative in a container of water and leave for another six minutes. Take it out of the water and, with your finger over the nozzle of the cold tap, clean off all the soap. The surface should be left smooth with no sign of soap, but try not to touch the surface. Put the plaster back in the empty container. Dilute about one dessertspoonful of detergent with a half a cup of water in a small jar and pour this over the surface. Turn the plaster over and leave to drain completely.

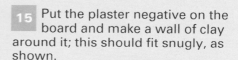

15 Put the plaster negative on the board and make a wall of clay around it; this should fit snugly, as shown.

16 Mix another batch of plaster and pour it over the negative mould, shaking the base lightly to minimise bubbles. The plaster should be no more than 5mm thick. Leave to set for about two hours. Make sure that the plaster is resting on a level surface as it sets, otherwise the thickness will be uneven.

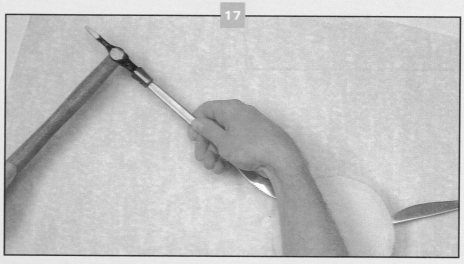

17 Take away the clay wall and with a small hammer wedge three table knives gently around the edge where you think the two plaster discs separate. Don't worry if they don't separate immediately; keep wedging the knives gently around the edge until they do.

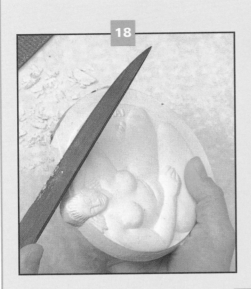

18 You now have a positive plaster image of your initial modelled design. Carefully cut away the extra plaster around the medallion, using a sharp knife and a rasp.

19 Use the rasp to remove some of the plaster from the back of the medallion. Sand the edges and back, using the method described in Step 3. Neaten up any defects with the modelling tools on the front of the medallion with modelling tools. Dry the plaster in a warm place for a day or two.

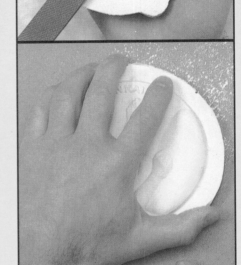

20 Put half a cup of shellac flakes in a jar and add one cup of methylated spirits. Leave to dissolve, then paint over the entire medallion. Allow to dry, then apply two more coats, drying between each application.

Now that you have learned the basic techniques for making a medallion, you may wish to use them to create another one with a more personal theme — perhaps a portrait of a family member or friend — or a small scene commemorating a special event in your family's life.

SCULPTURE AND 3-D

CAST BOOKENDS

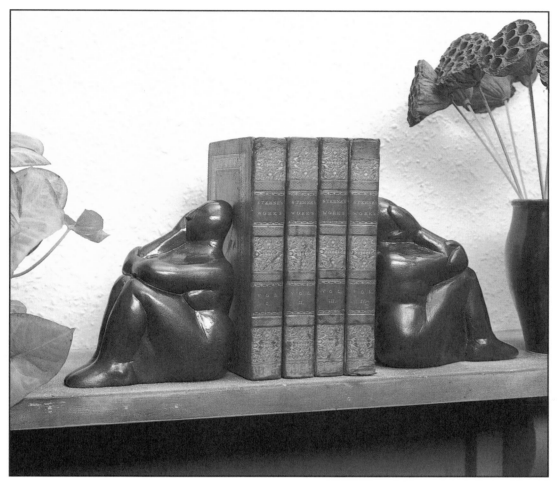

MATERIALS

To make the plaster bookends shown *below left* you will need:

Above, 5 kg clay; piece of board for rolling clay; sharp knife; assorted modelling tools; 2B pencil; roll of brass shim; scissors; double-sided sticky tape; polythene sheet; 3kg plaster of Paris; petroleum jelly; 3 kitchen knives; heavy-duty rubber band.

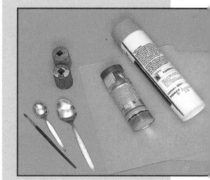

Above, size 2 paintbrush; teaspoon; dessertspoon; sandpaper in fine, medium and coarse grades; 2 lead sash window weights, each 1lb (available from builder's merchants); car body undercoat spraypaint; bronze metallic car spraypaint.

In this casting project we use clay to model the monumental seated figure from which our two attractive bookends are cast. A mould is then made and the figures are cast one by one in solid plaster and finished with bronze metallic paint. Each figure incorporates a hidden sash weight to make it heavy enough to act as an effective bookend.

As you will know if you made the Bas-relief medallion on page 31, the basic casting process consists of three stages. First a model is made — in this case, using clay; secondly a mould is made around the model (in this case using plaster of Paris); and thirdly the final object is cast in the mould.

Using clay to model the monumental shape of the seated figure for our cast bookends is wonderfully satisfying. Clay is easily sculpted using the fingers and modelling tools. The surface of the clay can be smoothed into sweeping curves with moistened fingers, and details can be picked out with pointed tools.

The mould of plaster of Paris is constructed with the help of a frame of brass shim. Plaster of Paris dries quickly and so is very suitable for this project in which the mould is built up in several stages. These must not be rushed, and the mould should not be moved or filled until the plaster has completely dried out.

Removing bubbles

Air bubbles are the greatest enemy in a project using plaster — if any are left in the mould they will weaken the finished sculpture. To avoid this happening make sure that the mould is kept moving while the plaster is being poured in. Placing a hand under the board and making a rapid up and down motion helps, as does rocking the mould from side to side before you leave the plaster to set.

HELPFUL HINT

You can buy modelling tools for plaster and clay, but many household items will do the same job. However, the one item you cannot do without is a sturdy plywood baseboard which has been sealed to prevent water absorption.

P R O J E C T

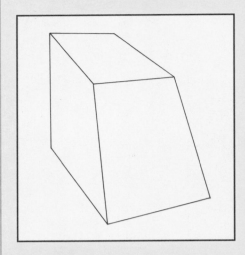

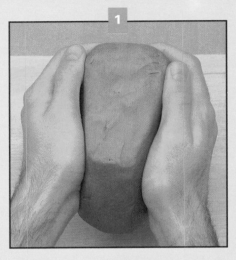

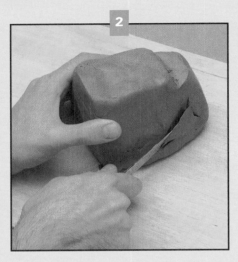

1 With the knife, cut off one-third of the clay and knead it on the board, shaping it with the hands into a wedge (see diagram, *above*). Drop the wedge on to the board to flatten the edges.

2 Use the knife to define the shape, cutting a step to form the top of the knees, gouging out a triangular cavity under them on both sides and sloping the shoulders down to the elbows.

3 Cut lines to demarcate the waist and arms. Blend and smooth the edges with your fingers as you work. Cut a slice downwards off the knees to make a sharp angle. Knead a small lump of clay into a square shape for the feet and attach to the base. Knead a lump of clay into a small oval for the head and attach to the shoulders.

4 Knead a small roll of clay for the raised arm and attach it to the right elbow. Attach to the head and mould the hand and thumb. With the thumbs and heels of the hands, shape and round the back of the figure, curving it into the base. Make sure the back remains perpendicular. Use a modelling tool to shape the detail of the feet and to define the nose.

HELPFUL HINT

If you find that the clay becomes too dry and brittle to mould easily, moisten your fingers with water as you work to make the clay more malleable.

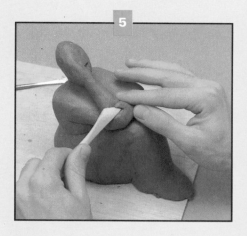

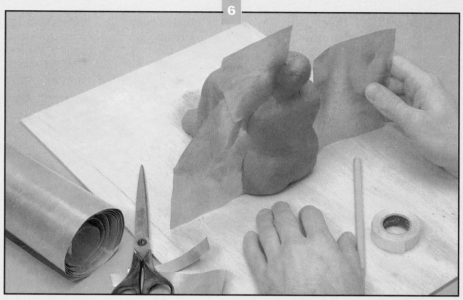

5 Use the fingers to mould the wedge shape where the hand meets the elbow and define the finger detail with a modelling tool.

6 With the pencil, draw round the base of the figure on the board. Use the scissors to cut a piece of shim approximately 6 x 10cm. Wedge it into the left side of the figure, pushing gently until it remains upright fixed in the clay. Trim off one corner with the scissors. Cut a piece of shim 6 x 6cm and wedge it into the shoulder and head of the figure, attaching it to the first piece with the double-sided sticky tape. Cut matching pieces of shim and wedge into the clay on the right side as you did on the left.

7 Make two thick rolls of clay and wedge them either side of the figure to make a seal between the shim and the board. Cover the front of the figure with a square of polythene, securing it to the shim with lumps of clay. Smear petroleum jelly where the model and the shim meet the board at the back.

8 Cover the work surface with the polythene sheet. Mix up the plaster in the plastic container, using the quantities given for the moulded tiles on page 29, and 'splat' it on to the back of the figure with your hands so that a fine layer covers the exposed surface.

9 Wait a few minutes until the plaster reaches a creamy consistency, then add more plaster until the plaster layer is about 3-4cm thick. Use the blade of the kitchen knife to smooth the surface.

10 When the plaster reaches a 'cheesy' consistency (about 20 minutes) clean any surplus plaster away from the base of the model with the knife. With the index finger, gouge out a groove round the plaster about 6cm up from the base (this is to provide a grip for the rubber band that holds the mould together). Leave to harden for at least two hours.

11 Remove the plastic sheet from the front of the model and gently pull away the shim additions. Use the modelling tool to gouge out eight small indentations for 'locating keys' at intervals around the side of the plaster mould.

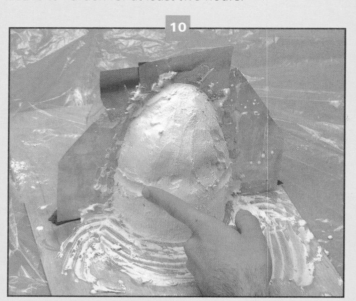

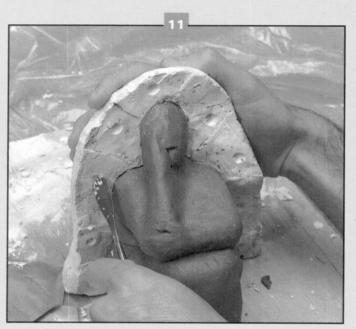

12 Coat the exposed plaster wall of the mould and all round the edges of the model, including the base, with petroleum jelly. With a small piece of clay, mould a rectangular plug and attach it to the the top of the figure's head against the side of the plaster mould. Cut a piece of shim 6 x 6cm and wedge up the centre of the front. Cut a piece of shim 4 x 4cm and wedge in to the elbow and arm, curving it to fit, and attaching to the first piece with the tape. Add more pieces of shim up to the clay plug.

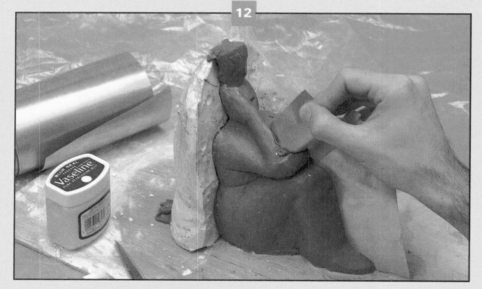

13 Seal to the board and protect the exposed side with polythene as in step 7. Repeat steps 8-11 for the lefthand front section of the mould. Then coat the exposed plaster walls with petroleum jelly as in step 12, and repeat steps 8-10 to make the final section. With the pencil, draw round the outside of the mould on the board.

14 Force open the mould by inserting the point of the knife in the seam and tapping with the hammer.

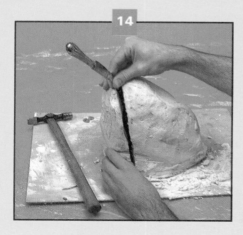

15 Clean the board. Clean the three sections of plaster mould under the tap to remove all traces of clay. Knead a small piece of clay to form an end piece 3cm deep for the weight and press the weight firmly on to it. Use the knife to smooth the edges and flatten the base. Using the pencil lines on the board as a guide, stick the weight in the centre of the widest part of the outline.

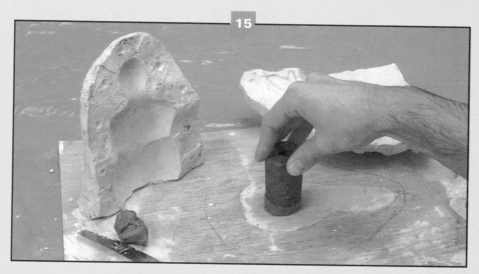

16 Use a metal modelling tool to gouge out a 1cm wide channel in one of the front sections of the mould (this is the air vent).

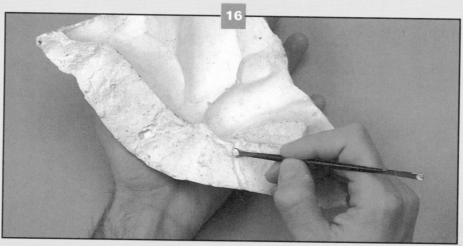

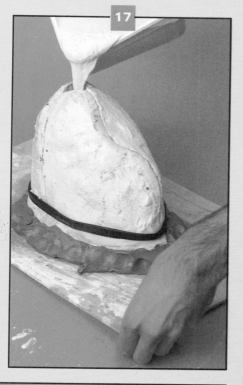

17 Apply petroleum jelly to all the inner surfaces of the mould, including the base and the walls. Place the sections together over the pencil marks on the board and hold in place with the elastic band. Put a thick roll of clay round the base of the mould, pressing it in position to seal the gap between the base and the board. Mix the plaster as before and pour through the opening in the top until completely filled. Place one hand under the board and shake it slightly while pouring in order to remove air bubbles. Leave to harden for at least two hours.

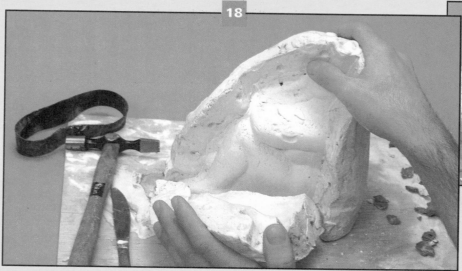

18 Remove the elastic band and use the hammer and knife to force open the mould. Carefully lever off the mould above the head.

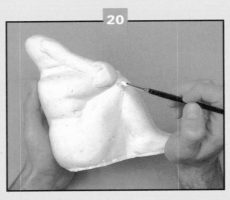

20 Immerse the plaster model in water. Mix up a small quantity of plaster on the teaspoon. Fill any holes or gaps with plaster using the paintbrush. Leave to harden.

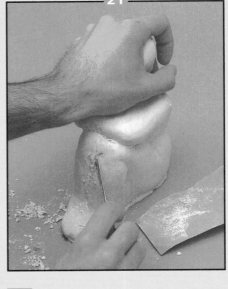

19 Remove the clay plug from the base of the figure. Mix a small quantity of plaster and spoon it into the cavity. Smooth over and leave to harden.

HELPFUL HINT

Using two different shades of bronze metallic paint will give an interesting two-tone effect to your sculpture.

21 Sand down any rough areas with the sandpaper. Use the modelling tool to define the detail of face, hands and the division of the lower legs.

22 Cover the work surface with the polythene sheet. Spray the model with a coat of the car body undercoat. Leave to dry for 15 minutes. If any uneven texture is revealed by this spraying, smooth with the sandpaper and spray again.

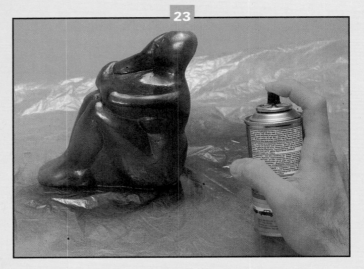

23 When thoroughly dry, spray with metallic bronze spraypaint. Leave to dry for 15 minutes. Repeat from step 15 to make the matching figure for the pair of bookends.

With their internal lead weights, your bookends will be solid and weighty but do take care — plaster is a brittle material and the figures will break if they are dropped.

SCULPTURE AND 3-D

PLASTER BIRD

MATERIALS

To make the plaster bird shown *below left* you will need:

Above, empty 1 litre fruit juice carton; 3kg plaster of Paris; wooden board; large plastic container; 1/2in chisel; hammer; sandpaper, fine, medium and rough; small kitchen knife (smooth blade); plaster knife; metal modelling tool for plaster, No 51; metal modelling tool for wax, No 117; large decorator's paintbrush; scissors; HB pencil; tablespoon; ruler.

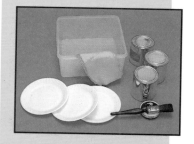

Above, water-soluble pigment powder: raw umber, burnt sienna, yellow ochre; 1in decorator's paintbrush; 3 plastic or ceramic plates; large container of water; neutral shoe polish; duster.

In this sculpture project we show you how to carve a form from a rectangular block of plaster. Our stylised bird is inspired by South American designs, and the finish is achieved with pigment stains and wax polish.

In this project we introduce you to the carving process, and show you how to sculpt a form 'freehand' from a solid rectangular block of plaster using various tools. The basic shape is roughed out with a chisel, which is tapped lightly with a hammer. Further carving is done with a plaster knife and a blunt, smooth-bladed kitchen knife. Modelling tools are used to define the details and to score the engraved lines. The pictures of the bird taken from different angles, along with diagram **3** on page 47, will help you to achieve the shape.

We have used a fruit juice carton to cast the block of plaster. As the carton is filled with plaster it bulges out slightly, resulting in a block with a slightly rounded contour which is appropriate for the subject. When the carton is removed from the plaster the closed end will have left a shallow V-shaped indentation which can be used as a guide when you come to carve the tail of the bird.

The plaster will be hard enough to work on within about two hours, and it is advisable to do the preliminary work before the plaster loses all its moisture and becomes too brittle. When you come to engraving and sanding, it is an advantage if the plaster is drier. Because plaster dries quickly it is essential to work fast, and a confident approach is vital. However, when using the hammer and chisel, don't drive the chisel too far into the plaster block as this may cause it to split in half.

When you have stained the bird with pigment, leave it to dry in a warm place for a couple of days before polishing it with wax to give it an attractive sheen.

HELPFUL HINT

The chisel, plaster knife and modelling tools are relatively inexpensive and can be obtained from most large art shops.

When carving a solid plaster block, keep the area being worked on damp to absorb impact and prevent fractures.

P R O J E C T

BASE TEMPLATE

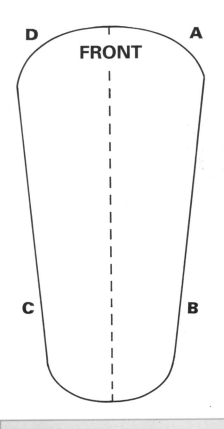

D ——— A

FRONT

C ——— B

1 Cut the top off an empty 1 litre fruit juice carton, then wash out the carton with clean water. Put 1 litre of water into a large plastic container and mix in plaster of Paris to the consistency of thick cream (see page 29). Pour the plaster into the carton to within 1cm of the top. Leave to set for at least two hours.

2 Tear the carton away from the plaster block. Photocopy the base template at the same size and cut out around the outline. Place the template on one of the long narrow sides of the block, lining up the front of the template with the straight end of the block (use the dotted line to centre the template). Draw around the template with a pencil, then use the sharp point of modelling tool 117 to score along the drawn line.

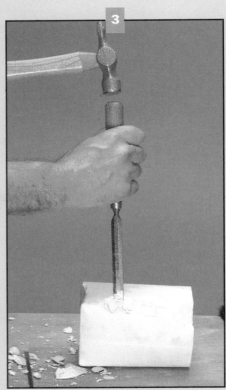

from the outline of the base to a depth of about 3cm to remove the corners. When you reach point **B** stand the block on end and carve around to point **C** with the chisel held at a shallower angle (about 30º). Carve from point **C** to point **D** with the chisel held at 60º. Brush away the plaster debris and dust with the large decorator's paintbrush.

3 Starting at point **A** shown on the base template, hold the chisel at an angle of about 60º and tap with the hammer to chip away

4 Turn the block over and sand the base smooth by rubbing it across a sheet of rough sandpaper. The shallow V-shape formed by the carton can be seen here.

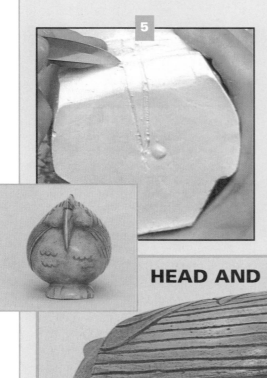

5 Score two lines 5mm apart down the centre of the other long narrow side (the top of the sculpture). Score another line at right angles to these, 2cm from the front edge, and using the hammer and chisel, carve down to a depth of 1cm along this line. Use the kitchen knife to shape the curved edge of the 'step' from which the beak will be shaped. On the front edge, mark and score two lines that meet at a point 4cm below the step (this will be the beak). Deepen the lines with the kitchen knife.

6 Chisel away the plaster from both sides of the beak to make a gently rounded contour, tapering the depth of cutting as you reach the end of the beak. Cut the plaster away from the outside of the two lines along the top, holding the chisel at an angle of 45°, and cut down to a depth of about 1cm, tapering to about 5mm at the tail end. With the chisel, carve away to the sides to achieve a roughly rounded shape, but avoid the area that will form the head at the top of the beak.

HEAD AND BACK

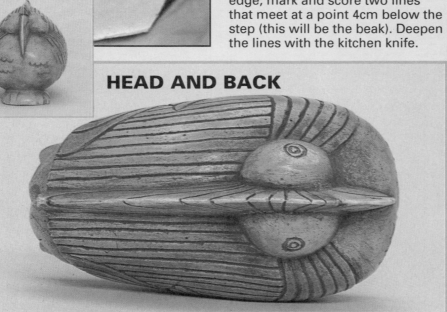

7 About 1cm from the base, scratch a line in the plaster all around the block and, using the kitchen knife and plaster knife, carve out the indent where the body meets the base. Chip away and scrape with the kitchen knife to form the profile of the head and back. Working all round the body, use the plaster knife to refine the contours. Here you can see the shape of the beak beginning to emerge.

8 With the two knives, carve and scrape the plaster to achieve rounded contours on the front and sides of the body. Create two sections of a sphere (with a diameter of about 4cm) on either side of the beak to form the head.

9 Define the beak and the crest with the knife, and when you are happy with the overall shape use the kitchen knife to smooth and refine all the contours.

diagram 1

4cm

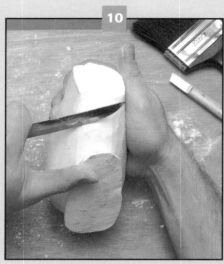

10 Mark a horizontal line on the tail end, 4cm from the base. Carve away this area with the chisel to the profile shown in diagram **1**. Use the knife to smooth and round off the contours.

11 Chisel another horizontal line across the tail end, 5cm from the base, and carve into the block to continue the profile as shown in diagram **2**. Smooth the shape with the knife.

TAIL END

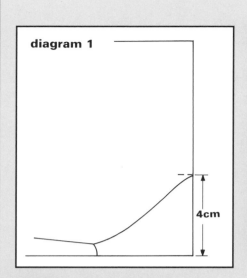

diagram 2

5cm

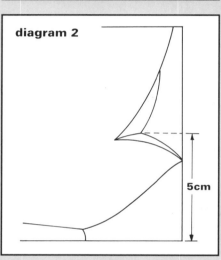

12 Use the knife to carve a V-shape into the end of the tail, using the line made by the seam on the carton as the centre point. Score a line to define the upper wing on both sides of the body, starting at the top of the crest 1cm from the back of the bird, gently curving down to a point near the base, then curving up again to the head.

13 Use the plaster knife to carve away the underwing to a depth of nearly 1cm at the top of the back, tapering down to 2mm near the base. Use the knife to smooth the surface.

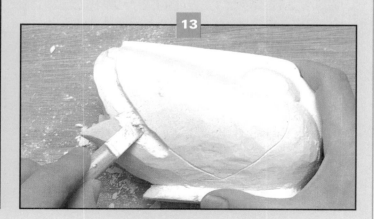

14 Score a second curved line starting from the point where the underwing and the tail meet and joining up with the line of the upper wing (see diagram **3**). Carve away the area below this line to a depth of 2mm and smooth off. Mark the curve of the bird's breast, and carve to a depth of 2mm. Smooth off.

15 Make a central V-shaped cut in the back of the underwing. Finish off the end of the bird's crest by cutting a small notch where it meets the wing.

16 Use the knife, modelling tools, sandpaper and your fingers to smooth and refine all the contours. Use small squares of sandpaper wrapped around your finger for shaping the intricate areas.

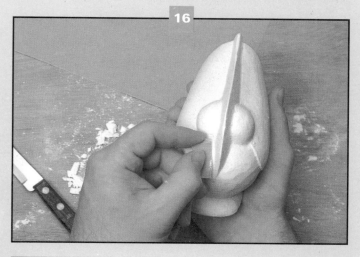

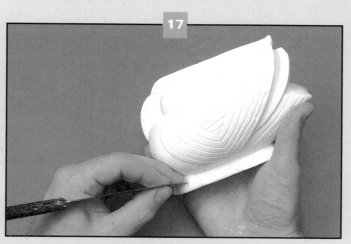

17 Using the pointed end of tool 51 and the knife, score all the lines and details (shown in red in diagram **3**).

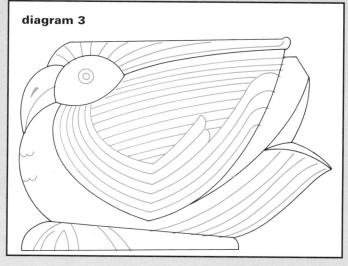

diagram 3

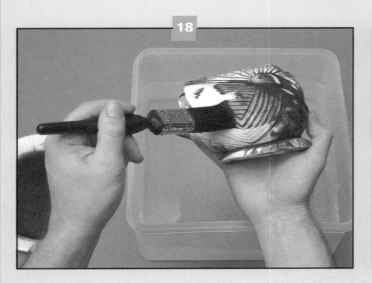

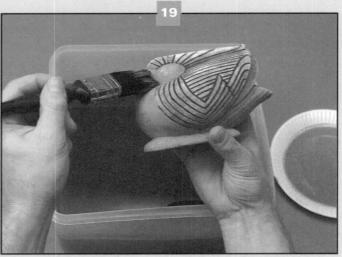

18 Take half a tablespoon of raw umber pigment and mix it on a plate with about 3 tablespoons of water (it should be the consistency of ink). Fill a container with water. Using the 1-inch decorator's brush, paint the whole bird, pushing the pigment into the engraved lines. Wash the bird immediately in the water; most of the paint will run off, leaving a light stain of colour. The engraved lines will appear darker.

19 Mix yellow ochre pigment on another plate, this time in a weaker solution. Apply this to all parts of the bird except the wings and crest. Wash off immediately as in step 18 to leave a light colour stain.

20 On a third plate, mix a weak solution of burnt sienna and apply it to the main wing and crest only. Wash off as before. If you prefer a darker colour repeat the painting and washing process.

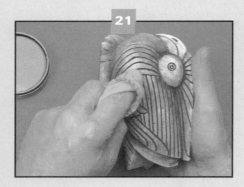

21 Leave the finished bird to dry for several days in a warm place. Apply a generous coat of neutral shoe polish with a soft duster. Leave for 10 minutes and then buff to a soft shine using a clean part of the duster.

Try using the basic techniques described in this lesson to produce your own design for a carved bird, animal or figure. You could use different-sized cartons — such as milk cartons — as moulds.

MODELLING

DRAPED FIGURE

MATERIALS

To make the figure shown *below left* you will need:

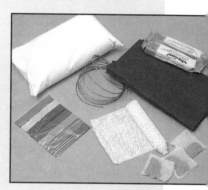

Above, 2.5kg bag of plaster of Paris; Gypsona fast-setting plaster of Paris bandage, 15cm wide; 30 x 74cm piece of coloured felt fabric; 125g plasticine; small pack of self-hardening clay; 1.5m length of galvanised wire (2.5mm diameter); 4 tea bags.

Above, pliers; ruler; scissors; sheet of plastic; measuring jug; large bowl; plastic bowl; small bowl; fine sandpaper; flat artist's paintbrush.

In a project inspired by classical stone sculptures, we show you how to create an elegant figure with flowing drapery using plaster-soaked fabric over a wire armature.

An armature made of steel, wood, wire netting or polystyrene is often used in modelling as a basic framework on to which the modelling material can be applied and which supports the whole structure.

In this project we use a galvanised wire armature for the basic shape, and this is then filled out with self-hardening modelling clay. The hands and head of the figure are built up with fast-setting plaster of Paris bandage (a loosely woven bandage with plaster incorporated which is used to encase broken limbs). The fabric is quite fine so is useful for building up fairly detailed areas. The natural-looking folds of

the gown are created by soaking felt fabric in plaster and modelling it on the figure.

Since plaster is a fast-setting material, the key to the project is speed. The setting action of plaster is not activated until you stir the mixture, so be sure that everything else is ready before you begin to prepare the plaster. The tea seems to slightly delay the setting time, but you will only have about five minutes in which to arrange the fabric. Make sure that the fabric is thoroughly covered — the dark colour will help you to see if it is. If you want to make this a solid sculpture, you must make sure that you seal the seams of the cloth.

HELPFUL HINT

You can buy the Gypsona fast-setting plaster of Paris bandages used in this project in most good specialist art and craft shops. Alternatively, make your own by soaking layers of scrim (an open weave fabric), or ordinary open-weave bandages, in plaster of Paris.

PROJECT

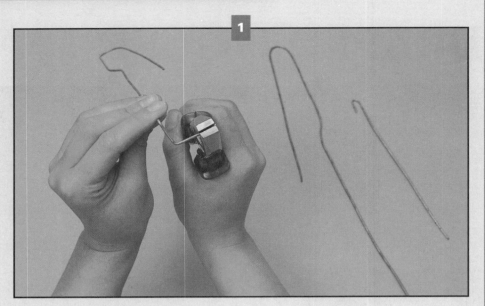

diagram 1

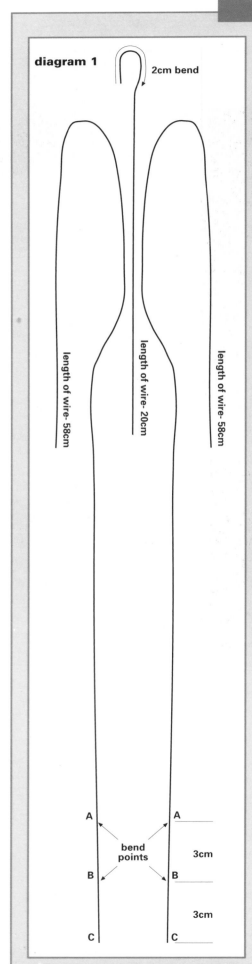

2cm bend

length of wire- 58cm

length of wire- 20cm

length of wire- 58cm

A   A

bend
points

B   B

3cm

3cm

C   C

1 Before you begin, make up
about three pints of tea with
four tea bags and leave to cool.
While it is cooling make the
armature. Cut two 58cm lengths of
wire and one 20cm length of wire.
Using diagram **1** as a guide, bend
them to shape with the pliers.
Make a tight curve at one end of
the short piece of wire. Bend the
curves in the long pieces of wire
following the diagram. Bend the
wires at points A and B as shown
in diagram **2**.

2 Shape the plasticine into a
rectangle measuring about 8 x
11cm, and about 2cm thick. Embed
the ends of the long wires in the
centre of the plasticine about 2cm
apart. Smooth the plasticine over
the wire to keep it in place.

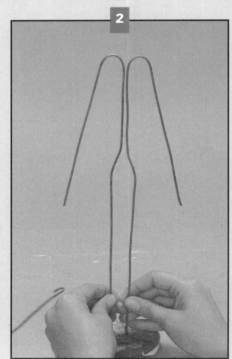

2

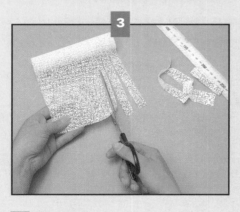

3

diagram 2

A

A

B

C

C

B

3 With scissors, cut about 20
strips 15 x 1cm of fast-setting
plaster of Paris bandage. Cut more
as you need them later.

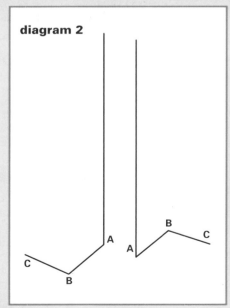

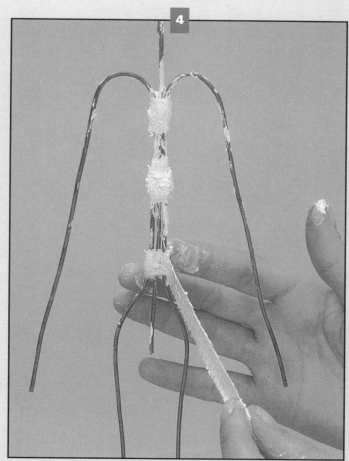

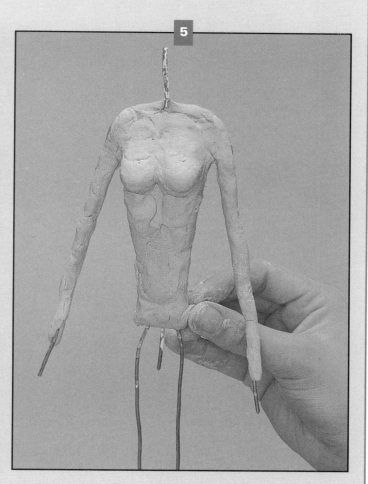

4 Cover the work surface with a sheet of plastic. Pour a little of the cold tea into a small bowl, dip one of the strips of bandage in it and, holding the central short piece of wire in place, wrap the bandage around the wires at the top to hold them together. Wrap a piece of the bandage around the middle and then at the bottom as shown.

5 Build up the shape of the torso and arms with the clay, applying pieces to either side of the armature to a depth of about 1.5cm. Build up the shape of the breasts. Roll little sausages of clay and wrap them around the wire to build up the arms a little, leaving about 2cm uncovered where the hands will be.

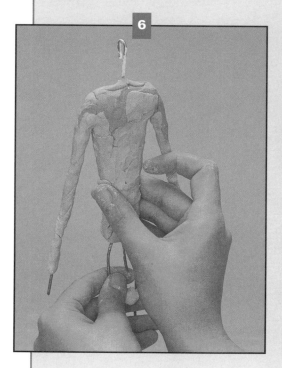

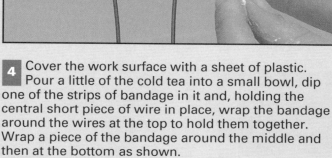

6 Build up the shape of the shoulders at the back.

7 Fold the piece of felt in half along the longest side and snip a 1cm slit in the centre of the fold.

8 Pour two pints of cold tea into a bowl and sprinkle plaster into it until the plaster 'peaks' above the surface (see page 29). Stir up the plaster when you are ready to work.

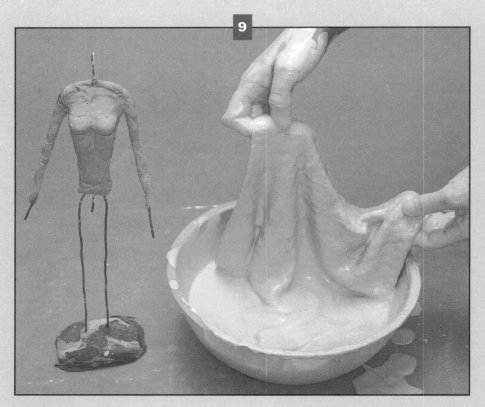

9 Dip the felt into the plaster and move it around until it is thoroughly covered. Place the armature on the plastic work surface and, holding the open ends of the felt, remove the fabric from the plaster.

10 Put the fabric on the armature, slipping the metal hook through the central slit. Pull the fabric into an A shape then start to arrange the folds, smoothing them with your hands. Make sure that the open seams on either side of the figure are folded in on each other (in the same way as a sewn seam) in order to seal them.

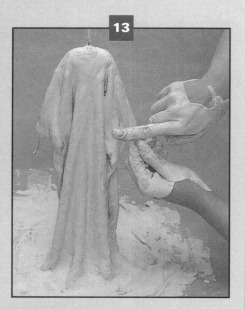

11 Use the flat brush to define and model the folds and cover the fabric, using the plaster from the work surface.

12 Arrange the fabric around the base of the figure, keeping the lines fluid. Pinch around the arms to define them, and pinch the seams together to seal them.

13 Smooth and model the shape with your fingers. Leave the plaster to dry for about 10 minutes. Remove from the sheet of plastic, and clean the plastic.

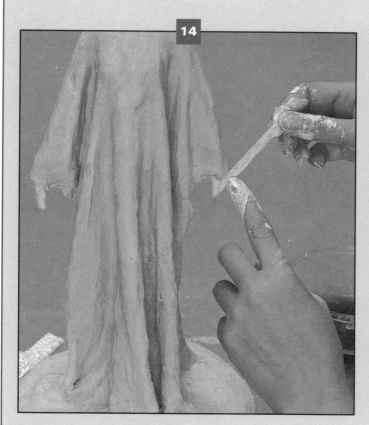

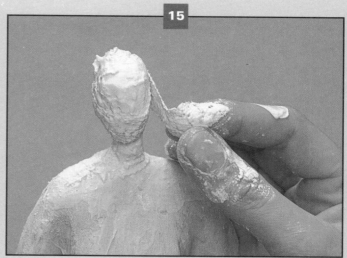

14 Place the figure back on the plastic. Dip a strip of bandage in cold tea and wrap it around the hands.

15 Wrap a piece of bandage around the wire hook at the top to form the neck and the core of the head. Then start to wrap pieces at the angle shown to form the shape of the head from the point of the chin to the back of the head, constantly moulding the shape with your fingers into a smooth ovoid shape.

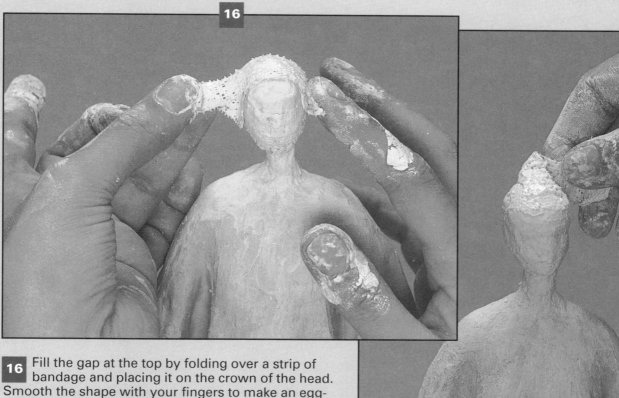

16 Fill the gap at the top by folding over a strip of bandage and placing it on the crown of the head. Smooth the shape with your fingers to make an egg-shaped head with a diameter of about 2.5cm.

17 Cut a couple of strips of bandage in half, dip in tea and place one end at the hair line. Take the rest up into a bun at the back of the head and smooth down.

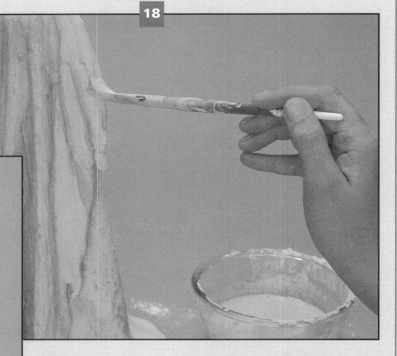

18 Mix up some fresh plaster with half a pint of tea in the same way as in step 8, and paint plaster on with the brush, making sure that the fabric is completely covered, and smoothing the surface with your fingers.

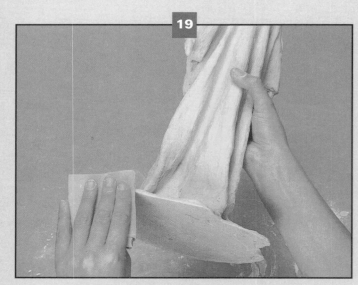

19 Leave the figure to dry overnight. With a small piece of sandpaper, smooth off any lumps. Sand the base so that the figure stands firmly.

The tea in the plaster mix imparts a pinkish-brown hue to the figure which gives it some warmth. You could add more colour by dabbing a cold wet tea bag on to some of the folds. After a couple of weeks, when the figure is completely dry, you can rub some clear wax polish over the surface to protect it and give it a subtle sheen.

MODELLING

COILED CLAY POT

MATERIALS

To make the clay pot shown *below left* you will need:

Above, 5kg raku clay; banding wheel or whirler; sheet of hardboard (or wooden work surface).

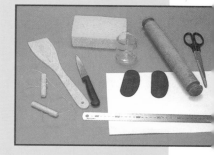

Above, smooth metal kidney; serrated metal kidney; clay cutting wire; small piece of paper; pointed, smooth-bladed kitchen knife; wooden rolling pin; wooden kitchen spatula; sponge; small jam jar; scissors; ruler.

In this modelling project we show you how to handbuild a clay pot using the ancient technique of coiling, and how to build up low relief decoration.

Pottery is often thought of as a highly sophisticated craft which uses much technical equipment, and which requires extensive training and a knowledge of complicated chemical processes. But the joy of it is that you can actually make lovely functional or decorative objects with very little technical experience or training.

Natural earth clays come in many different varieties, all of which must be fired in a kiln to harden them (known as biscuit firing); and if they are then glazed they must be fired again. We have used raku clay, which is good for handbuilding because it contains a good deal of grog (ground up highly fired clay) which adds body to the clay. It is also relatively inexpensive. Raku

clay requires little preparation before working. If you are using a different type of clay you may need to wedge it (cut off a piece of clay and slap it down on a table to expel any air bubbles) to make it workable.

Coiling can be done in one of two ways: either by rolling out a sausage of clay and building up the structure with a continuous spiral coil of clay, or by making individual coils, or rings, of clay and joining the pieces together, which is the technique we have used in the project.

Leave the pot to dry thoroughly before firing it or it may explode. Kilns are expensive pieces of equipment, so try to find a potter who will let you use theirs, or try an adult education centre.

HELPFUL HINT

Adult education centres running pottery courses will advise you on how to get your pot fired, and may even let you use their own kiln if they have one and it is not too much in demand. Otherwise, ring your local pottery suppliers.

P R O J E C T

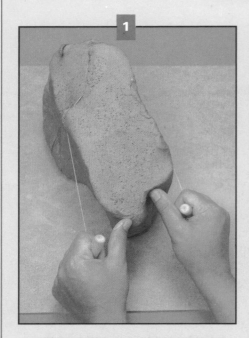

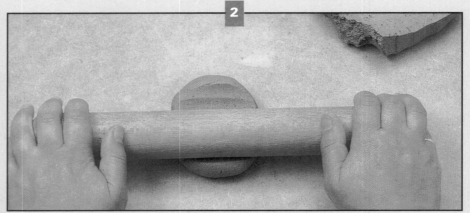

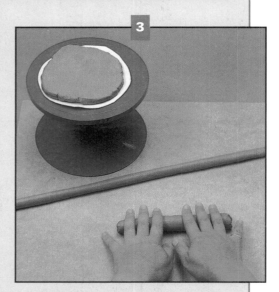

1 Work on a wooden or plastic work surface or board. Slice off a piece of clay by pulling the nylon cutting wire through it.

2 Take a handful of clay, roll it into a ball and then roll out with a rolling pin to a thickness of 1.5cm, to make a circular slab about 12cm in diameter.

3 Cut a piece of paper to a circle roughly 14cm diameter and place on the banding wheel. Put the clay slab on it. Roll another piece of clay into a ball, then roll out into a long sausage shape as shown, until about 1.5cm in diameter. Make more 'sausages' as needed.

HELPFUL HINT

Keep unused clay in a plastic bag, and always cover your work with a sheet of plastic to keep it malleable. Store any unused clay in a well-sealed plastic bag in a cool, frost-free place out of direct sunlight.

HELPFUL HINT

It is best to use one sausage for each coil, although you can join them more than once if you need to. Make sure that the clay is solid and that no air bubbles are left in the join. If the sausage begins to flatten and rolls unevenly, pinch into shape and then continue rolling. When joining the coils, stagger the position of the joins on the pot so that you do not end up with an area of weakness in one part of the pot. The banding wheel, which rotates freely, will help you to work on the piece, but is not essential.

4 Cut one end off one of the sausages, coil it round until you have a circle about 10cm in diameter, cut off the other end and join the ends together, smoothing the join with your fingers. Score the slab with the serrated kidney in the area where the clay coil will go, then put it in place and smooth the join on the inside with your fingers.

5 With the serrated kidney, roughen the surface of the top of the coil. Cut another sausage approximately to length, and place it on the middle to outside edge of the first coil. Trim the sausage to fit, join neatly, then smooth the joins on the inside.

6 Continue building up the coils, placing them on the outside edge of the previous one, and making them gradually larger so that the shape of the pot grows. After about four more coils, smooth down the inside of the pot with your fingers to strengthen the whole structure.

7 Cut away the excess clay from around the bottom of the pot with a knife, and smooth.

8 Smooth the surface of the coils on the outside of the pot with your fingers.

9 Continue building up and outwards with further coils, smoothing the inner and outer surfaces, until you reach the widest point (at a height of about 12cm). Leave to dry overnight. With the serrated kidney, scratch the top and attach a coil slightly on the inside of the rim (the shape will now narrow and the coils will be progressively slightly shorter).

10 Continue building the pot, smoothing the joins on inside and outside as you work. Stop when the pot is about 20cm high and the opening about 8cm wide.

11 With the serrated kidney, scrape the shape smooth.

MAKING SLIP

When you are joining new clay to old clay you must use slip to bind them together. To make slip, put a little clay in a small jam jar and add a little water to make a 'buttery' mixture. Apply this to the pot with your fingers or a knife.

12 With the wooden kitchen spatula, bat the pot into shape (lift it so that you can bat the base into shape). Leave to dry overnight to become leather-hard (partially dry but still workable).

13 With a sharp knife, trim around the opening of the pot. Make a coil to fit around the opening. Score the edge of the opening with the serrated kidney, smear some slip (see Making slip, *left*) over the opening, then fit the coil on top.

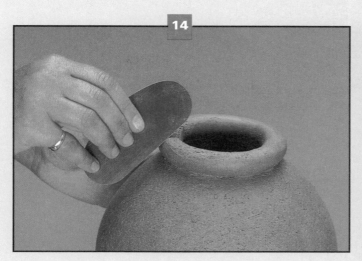

14 Smear a little more slip into the join on the inside and outside of the coil, filling any holes or cracks in the join. When the slip has dried, trim away the excess and scrape the coil with the kidney to give it an even shape.

15 Enlarge the lizard templates on a photocopier at 200%. Cut around the outline of one template, dampen the paper to make it more flexible and place in position on the pot. With the pointed knife, scratch into the pot around the outline. Repeat with the other lizard template on the other side of the pot.

TEMPLATES

16 Scrape the area marked out for one of the lizards with the serrated kidney. With your finger or a knife, smear some slip on to the lizard shape, and build up the shape in low relief by adding small lumps of clay. Model the shape with your fingers, making it thicker along the spine and centre of the legs.

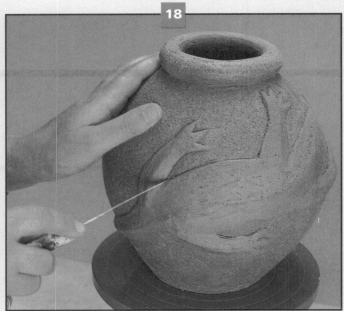

17 When you are happy with the general shape, use the smooth kidney to define the fluid curve of the ridge of the spine and smooth the shape of the legs and head. This will also give the surface of the modelling a uniform roughened surface.

18 With the knife, define the outline of the shape. Finally, add the eyes.

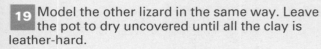

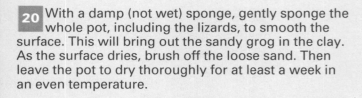

19 Model the other lizard in the same way. Leave the pot to dry uncovered until all the clay is leather-hard.

20 With a damp (not wet) sponge, gently sponge the whole pot, including the lizards, to smooth the surface. This will bring out the sandy grog in the clay. As the surface dries, brush off the loose sand. Then leave the pot to dry thoroughly for at least a week in an even temperature.

The dry pot can now be fired in an electric kiln at a temperature of about 950°C. It will change colour and take on a texture rather like that of sandstone, and it will also shrink slightly. The fired pot can be used as it is, in its natural biscuit-fired state, or you can decorate the surface with glazes (which will require another firing), or more simply with paint. If you paint rather than glaze the pot, don't use water in it, as an unglazed biscuit-fired pot is slightly porous and the painted decoration will be spoiled.

MODELLING

CANDLEHOLDERS

In this modelling project we show you how to make a pair of unusual candleholders. Our charming clay horses are modelled in the traditional style of South American pottery, which is first biscuit-fired and then hand-painted.

In our coiled clay pot project (see page 55) we used raku clay, which is suitable for hand-building because it contains grog (ground-up highly fired clay). For this project we are using a clay called 'T material', which is more appropriate for smaller, sculptural pieces. 'T material' is similar to raku clay but is a little more expensive because it contains an even higher proportion of grog and has a finer texture. It is very easy to work with and keeps its shape well, even when in the malleable state.

Eliminating air pockets
As with any highly grogged clay, it is not necessary to 'wedge' T material (slamming it repeatedly on a table to expel air pockets). However, it is very important to

make sure that no air is trapped in the body of the clay as you build up the form, as this can cause the clay to crack, or even explode, during firing.

As a rule, solid sculptures must be hollowed out before they have dried so that the 'shell' of clay is not more than 2.5cm thick; this ensures that they do not break during firing (if the form is too thick it will dry and fire unevenly). However, in this project we fire the whole solid form, and for this reason it should not be made any larger than the given dimensions. As a precaution small holes are pierced in the thickest parts of the form to allow any trapped air to escape during firing, and it should be biscuit-fired slowly, the temperature of the kiln being built up gradually to a temperature of 950ºC.

MATERIALS

To make the clay candleholders shown *below left* you will need:

Above, approximately 5kg of T material clay; banding wheel or whirler; nylon cutting wire; pottery knife; piercing tool; wooden modelling tool; bowl of water; latex sponge; piece of foam rubber approximately 15 x 10cm; jam jar.

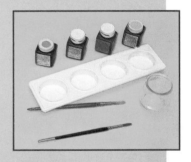

Above, acrylic paints, rouge, russet, Pacific sky and bluestone; paintbrushes: round soft hair sizes 10 and 6; mixing palette; jar of water.

HELPFUL HINT

When modelling in clay, rather than just using it for moulds, use the best quality clay available. It is usually sold in plastic bags, and will keep for long periods if kept sealed. This means you can buy in bulk to keep costs down.

PROJECT

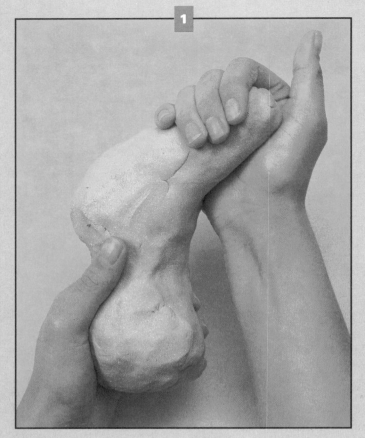

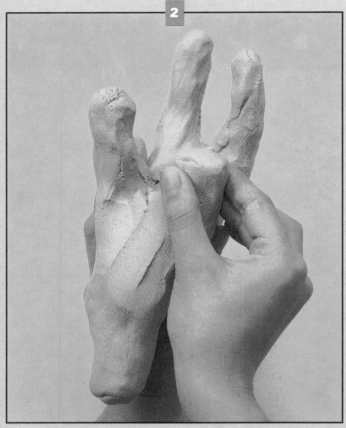

1 Slice off a piece of clay, about 2kg in weight, by pulling the nylon cutting wire through it. Roughly form the clay into a long 'loaf' shape, then pull it upwards at one end to begin forming the horse's neck. Make the body about 13cm long and the neck about 16cm long, measured from the base of the body.

2 Pull the clay out from the base of the body to shape the legs, making them about 8cm long.

HELPFUL HINT

The instructions given are for one candleholder — to make a pair, simply make a second one as you go along. The measurements are an approximate guide only. They are slightly larger than the finished form to allow for later refining of the model and for 10% shrinkage during firing.

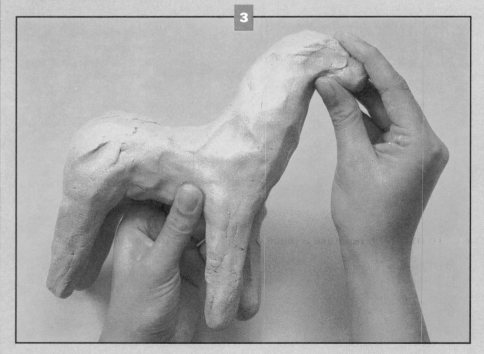

3 Form the head by pulling the top of the neck out and slightly down. Model the head into a slightly tapering 'sausage' shape, about 6cm long from the nose to the back of the neck.

4 With the tips of your fingers, pull the clay up from the back of the neck to form the ears.

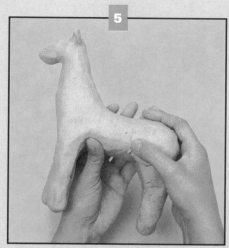

5 Use your fingers to refine the shapes of the body and limbs, still retaining the sturdy, stocky character of the horse. Take a small piece of clay and use this to fill out the horse's rump, smoothing the edges of the new piece into the surrounding clay with your thumb. Repeat for the other rump.

6 Stand the horse on the banding wheel and wedge the piece of foam rubber under its belly to stop it sagging. With the flats of your thumbs, press into the backs of the legs, about halfway up, to form the hocks.

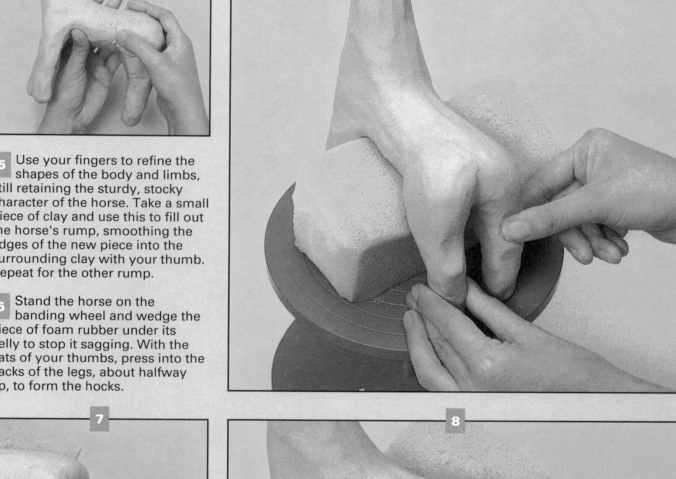

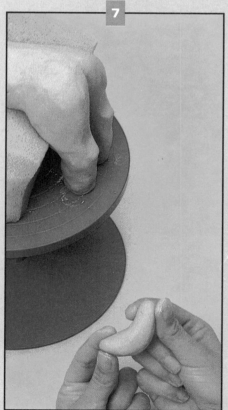

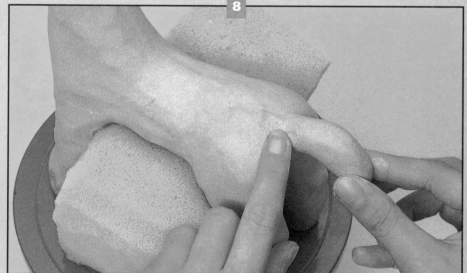

7 To make the tail, take a piece of clay 7cm long and roll it into a sausage shape, slightly thicker in the middle, then bend it slightly.

8 Press the tail into place, smoothing the clay of the tail into the clay of the body to obtain a good contact. Leave overnight, or until the clay has dried leather hard (partially dry but still impressionable), with the piece of foam rubber still in place.

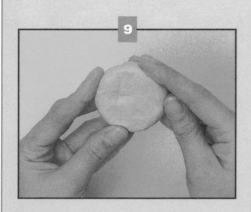

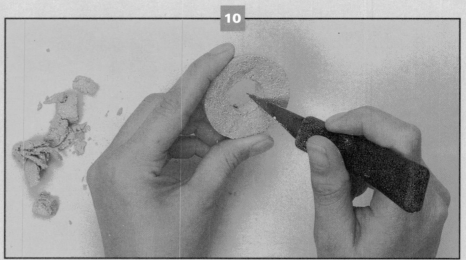

9 To make the candleholder, take a piece of clay and form it into a circle 5.5cm in diameter and 2.5cm deep.

10 With the pottery knife, make a hole in the centre of the candleholder. The diameter of the hole should be 10% larger than the diameter of your chosen candle (to allow for shrinkage of the clay during firing). Chamfer the outer sides of the candleholder inwards to form it into a shallow bowl shape. Leave to dry leather-hard.

11 Hold the horse in one hand and use the pottery knife to carve and smooth it into a more slender and elegant outline. Do the same with the candleholder.

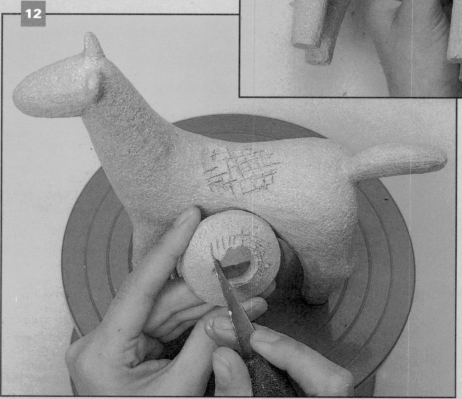

12 Now the candleholder can be attached to the horse's back. For this you will need some slip to bind the two pieces together. Put a little clay in a small jam jar and add enough water to make a 'buttery' mixture. With the pottery knife, score the base of the candleholder and the area of the horse's back where the holder is to be placed (in the middle, so that the rim of the holder almost touches the neck).

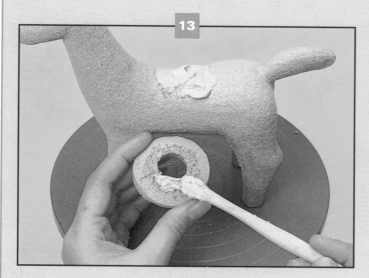

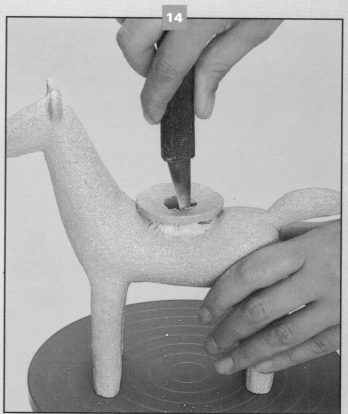

13 Using the wooden modelling tool, smear the slip over the scored areas and press the candleholder in place on the horse's back. Leave the slip to dry slightly.

14 Holding the pottery knife vertically inside the candleholder, extend the hole in the candleholder into the horse's back by a further centimetre, so that it provides support for the candle. Smooth the hole with your fingertip. Leave until the slip is leather-hard.

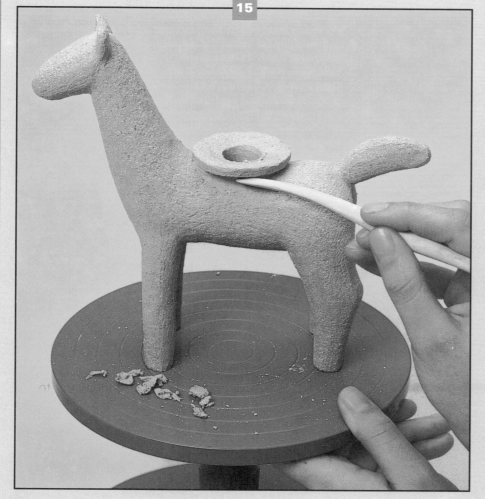

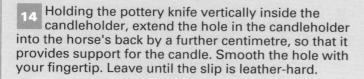

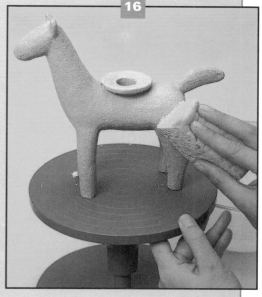

15 With the pottery knife, trim away the excess slip under the candleholder, then smooth the area with the modelling tool.

16 Dip the latex sponge in water, wring it out and gently wipe it over the whole surface of the piece to take away the knife marks and produce a smooth finish. This will bring up the grog in the clay. As the surface dries, brush off the loose sand.

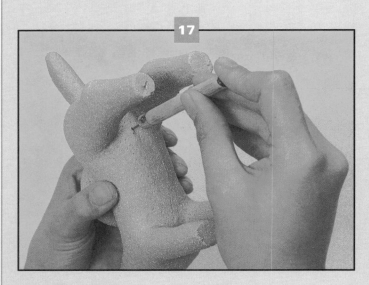

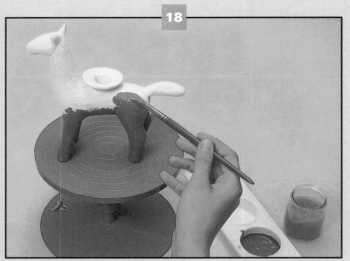

17 Use the piercing tool to make holes in the thickest parts of the horse's body (under the belly, in the chest and beneath the tail), pushing the blade of the tool in as far as it will go. This allows air to escape from the clay during firing. Leave to dry thoroughly before getting the pieces biscuit-fired (see Helpful Hint, *below right*). Arrange for the firing to be done slowly to ensure that the thicker parts are properly fired.

18 When the work has been fired, it is ready for painting. Create a terracotta colour from a 50-50 mix of rouge and russet acrylic paints, and a pale blue from a 50-50 mix of Pacific sky and bluestone. The paint should be the consistency of thin cream. Paint the body of the horse — except the ears and tail — and the inside of the candleholder terracotta, using the size 10 brush.

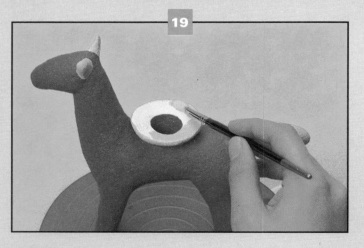

HELPFUL HINT

You can probably get your work fired at a local pottery, or perhaps a local pottery evening class. Make sure your work is thoroughly dry before it is biscuit-fired, otherwise it may fracture or even explode in the kiln. Drying will take at least a week in a warm room — and longer if the room is cold. You will know when the clay is dry because it will become lighter in colour and no longer feel cold to the touch — the cold is a sign of dampness.

19 With the blue mix and the size 6 brush, paint the horse's ears and tail, and the rim and sides of the candleholder. The paint dries quickly due to the porosity of the surface — if it goes streaky, apply a second coat.

Painted in simple colours, the finished piece has an appealing, 'naive' quality. Alternatively, you could further decorate the horse with painted patterns, which is another feature of South American pottery.

MODELLING

CLAY HEAD

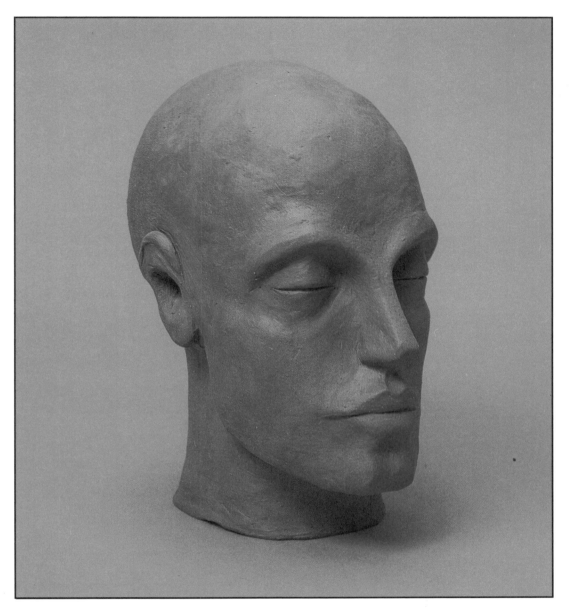

MATERIALS

To make the clay head shown *below left* you will need:

Above, 5kg prepared grey clay; 20cm length of 3 x 3cm softwood; blockboard 30 x 30cm; 2 corner braces and screws.

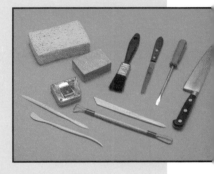

Above, solid hardwood modelling tools and wire-ended modelling tool; palette knife (optional); screwdriver; large kitchen knife; sponge; small block of wood; decorator's brush; tape measure.

In this final project in our introduction to modelling, we show you the basic method used by sculptors for modelling a head in clay. The finished head is hollowed out before firing to ensure that it does not explode in the kiln.

Most people who work with clay want to attempt a human head at some time or other. This project shows you how to model a stylised head — once you understand the basic method you can then attempt a likeness of a friend.

To support the clay while you are working on it, a simple wooden armature is constructed on the blockboard. While modelling the head, look in a mirror and feel your own head with your hands to get an idea of the shape of the cranium and facial features. It is important to keep the clay damp while you are working on it (see page 68). If you have to leave the work for any period of time, cover it with a damp cloth and a plastic bag.

When the modelling is finished the head has to be cut open and hollowed out. This may seem rather alarming, but it is essential if the piece is to be fired. After hollowing out the two pieces are joined together again and the head is left to dry in a temperate room (away from draughts and direct heat) for about 10 days. When the head is dry you can take it to a commercial kiln for firing.

PROJECT

1 Make the armature by fixing the length of softwood to the blockboard base with the angle braces as shown.

HELPFUL HINT

It is important to work all round the sculpture as it progresses. Turn the board frequently, or use a banding wheel.

2 Take a handful of clay and mould it into a slightly flattened shape, pressing out any air bubbles. Wrap it around the base of the wooden armature, pressing it on firmly. Continue to build up the shape on the armature.

3 Continue building up layers of clay until the shape measures about 32cm in circumference (this will be the thickness of the neck), and about 23cm in height.

HELPFUL HINT

To stop the clay drying out, spray it occasionally with a fine mist of water (a small handheld spray is useful). If you stop work on the piece, even for a very short period of time, cover it with a damp cloth and a plastic bag to keep it moist and workable, and keep it in a cool place.

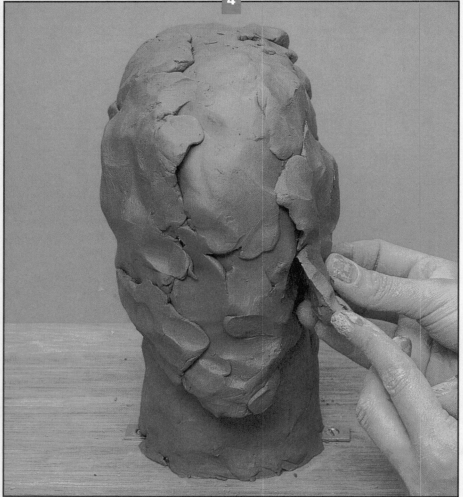

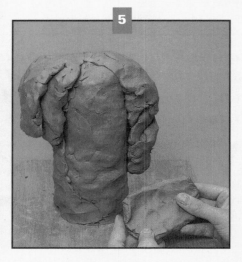

4 Build up the clay to form the front and back of the cranium, and the chin, as shown.

5 Build up the sides of the cranium to round out the shape a little, then begin to smooth down the clay and to model the form of the head all round with your fingers.

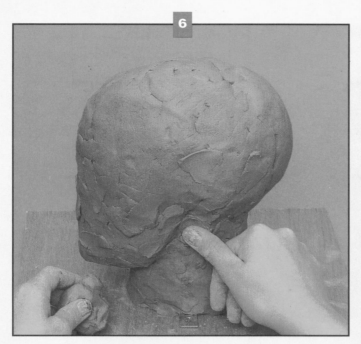

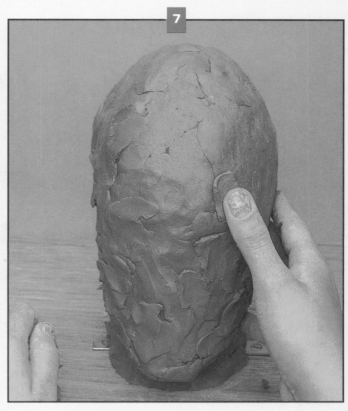

6 Begin to model and refine the shape of the sides of the head, defining the jaw line, smoothing the shape with your fingers and modelling tools, and adding small pieces of clay where necessary.

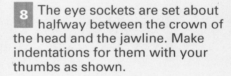

7 Continue refining the shape of the head, and begin to smooth the surface of the clay with your fingers.

8 The eye sockets are set about halfway between the crown of the head and the jawline. Make indentations for them with your thumbs as shown.

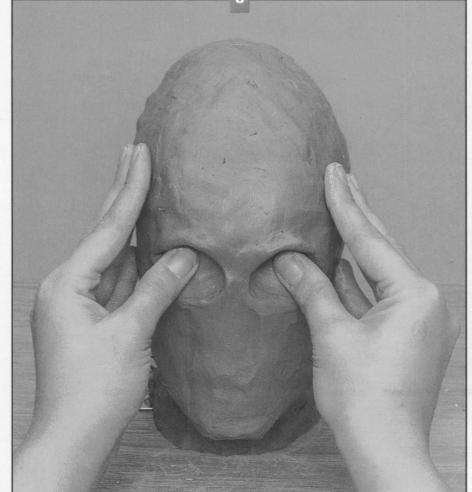

9 Using the small block of wood, start to pat the head into shape to simplify it into a more stylised form.

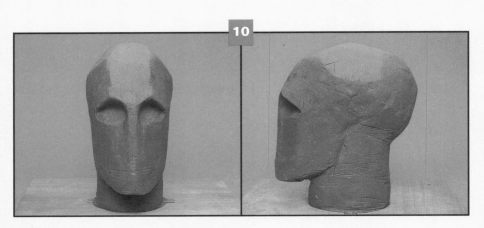

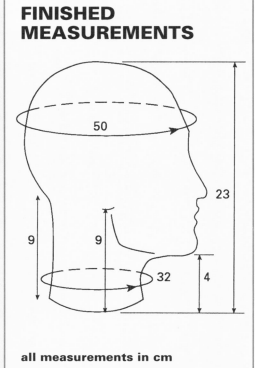

FINISHED MEASUREMENTS

50

23

9

9

32

4

all measurements in cm

10 Continue patting the head into shape, emphasising the facial and cranial planes, using the photographs *above* and the diagram *far right* as a guide.

11 Score a line down the centre of the face and mark approximately the position of the base of the nose and the mouth. Model a wedge-shaped piece of clay for the nose.

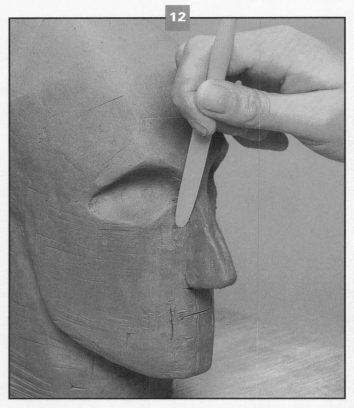

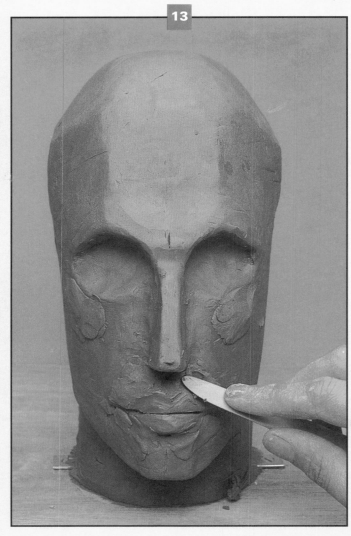

12 Stick the nose in position and smooth down the edges with a modelling tool and your fingers.

13 Apply additional pieces of clay to the cheeks. Roll out small pieces for the upper and lower lips and apply them, then apply more clay above and below the lips to build up the shape. Model the forms and define the shapes with the modelling tool.

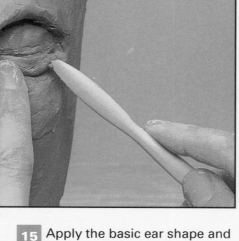

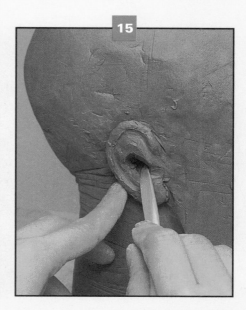

14 Roll small shapes to form the upper and lower eyelid, apply to the eye sockets, pressing them on firmly, and model to shape.

15 Apply the basic ear shape and smooth down the join at the front of the head. Push the modelling tool behind the ear to join part of the back of it to the skull. Model a channel to form the rim of the ear and gouge out the hole as shown.

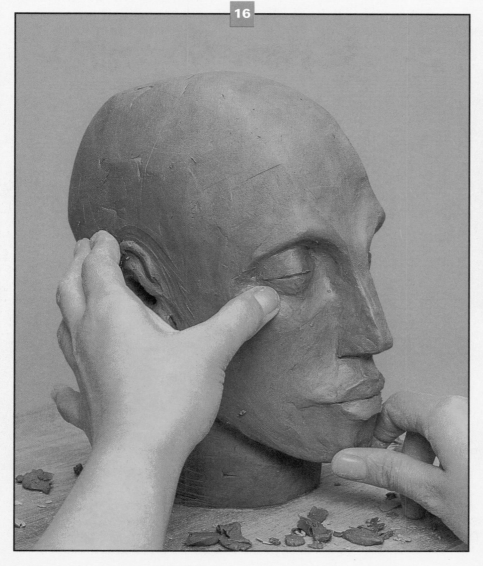

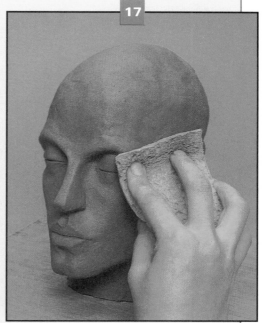

16 Continue refining the features of the face, modelling the cheekbones, cheeks and shape of the nose, and smoothing the surface.

17 With a damp sponge, dab the surface of the head and neck to give it a slight texture.

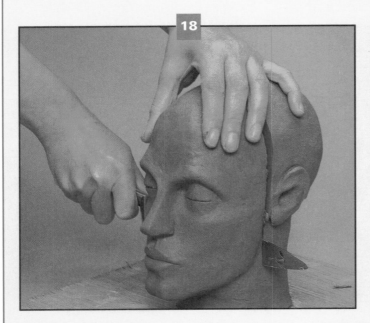

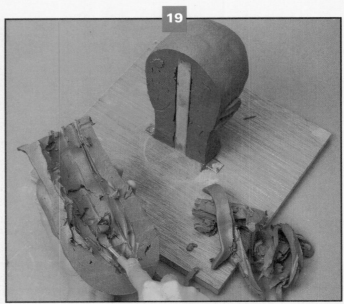

18 Leave the sculpture to dry uncovered until it is leather hard. With a large sharp kitchen knife (or cutting wire), make a cut right through the head just in front of the ear (cutting just to one side of the wood post).

19 Carefully prise away one half of the head and, with the wire loop, begin to take out the clay from the centre of the head to within about 2.5cm of the edge. As you go deeper into the clay, work very carefully to avoid removing too much.

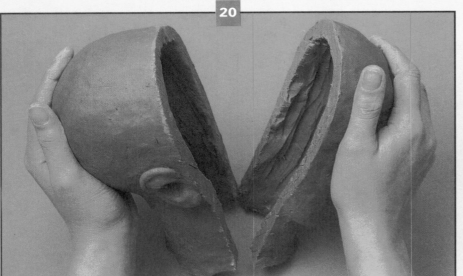

20 Remove the other half of the head from the wood support and hollow out the clay. Score the cut edges with the palette knife. Moisten the edges with a wet brush and some thin slip (see page 60). Press the two halves firmly together.

21 With your fingers, smooth the join in the clay.

Leave the sculpture to dry out thoroughly for a week or more before having it fired. If you wish, you can leave the piece as it is — it will remain stable for a considerable time without firing.